# DOGECOIN IN A NUTSHELL

THE DEFINITIVE GUIDE TO INTRODUCE YOU TO THE WORLD OF DOGECOIN, CRYPTOCURRENCIES, TRADING AND MASTER IT COMPLETELY

## SEBASTIAN ANDRES

WB PUBLISHING

# CONTENTS

# HOW TO USE THE BOOK

## How to use the book

First of all I would like to thank you for your trust and for choosing me as your guide to embark on this journey into the world of Cryptocurrencies. This book will help you to understand and master this world with the objective of obtaining an excellent financial education through the comprehension and understanding of Cryptocurrencies. In this book we will go from the most basic to the most advanced.

We understand that entering the world of cryptocurrencies can be tedious and very slow because there is a lot of information that we must understand and assimilate, usually the pioneers in this type of technology are people who have no problem to generate passive income online because they have some basic knowledge of this world that can help them a lot. The purpose of this book is that you can also shorten this path and have the knowledge in time to take advantage of them, as you know the world of cryptocurrencies moves very quickly and you can not waste time.

This technology is here to stay and to give us, the ordinary people, more economic and financial freedom.

In my experience, one of the things that caught my attention when I became interested in cryptocurrencies back in 2011, was the concept of freedom that is related to currencies such as Bitcoin, Monero, Dash, Zcash, etc. where the control of the whole process always goes by hand with the user because of the privacy they provide. Don't worry, you will understand these concepts later on during the development of the book.

In this book I will teach you the different approaches to Cryptocurrencies and the technology behind it: starting from the actual concept of money to the Blockchain, why it works, what is the secret behind it and we will also debunk some myths related to some concepts.

The objective of this book is to teach you to have a more complete and complex notion about Cryptocurrencies, from the most basic concepts such as knowing how everything works, how the pieces fit together, to the most advanced.

I have also taken the time to suggest some resources to get you started on the right foot. Keep in mind that many of these links are affiliate links, so you will receive some discounts and benefits by using the referred link, at no cost to you. So take advantage of it.

I wrote this book not only to inform you about the world of cryptocurrencies but also to motivate you to take that step that is so hard for you and take action, that is why I want to ask you one thing, do not give up throughout this book, follow the advice at your own risk, I promise you that by finishing this book and applying step by step my advice and teachings you will be able to better understand this world and according to your personal actions achieve financial freedom or also support this initiative that gives power to us citizens against the current financial system that is too manipulated and makes a few people rich.

Again, thank you very much for purchasing this book, I hope you enjoy it.

# ABOUT ME

## Why should you listen to me?

Greetings, my name is Sebastian Andres, I am an entrepreneur, writer and world traveler. I am a cryptocurrency enthusiast since 2011 when I started to get interested in this world. I feel extremely blessed to have been born in this era, and to be able to experience the growth of these technologies such as the internet and cryptocurrencies.

For more than 10 years I have focused on developing several internet businesses, which taught me to develop my own strategies and methods to generate passive income. Cryptocurrencies was one of them and that is how I achieved financial freedom.

The purpose of my books, more specifically of the collection "Cryptocurrency Basics" (in which I bring the most current and reliable information on cryptocurrencies, if you are interested you can look for the other books in this collection, in which we address other cryptos) is to be a source of inspiration for you and generate a change in those who are not satisfied with the established and know that they can give more, that they can generate a positive change in their lives and get to design that lifestyle they want so much.

I am confident that this information will help you to get that final jump start and get into cryptocurrencies in depth.

# DISCLAIMER

Important

Investing in financial markets such as cryptocurrencies and other assets can lead to money losses. The purpose of this book is only educational and does not represent an investment advice, for that there are already many professionals in the area that can help you. Proceed with caution, at your own risk and remember, never invest more than you are willing to lose.

**By continuing to read this book you accept this Warning.**

# ONE

# DOGECOIN, FROM A MEME TO THE BEST INVESTMENT OF 2021

Let's start by saying that Dogecoin is a cryptocurrency based on one of the most famous memes of all time. Surprisingly, its comical nature has not hurt its survival. It has a dedicated community of users who have raised funds for a number of initiatives over its few years of existence.

The advent of Bitcoin in 2009 opened the floodgates for digital currencies. Since its launch, thousands of alternative cryptocurrencies or altcoins have emerged to suit a wide range of use cases. Some seek to establish themselves as money, while others aim to power smart contract platforms such as Ethereum. Among the above coins, Dogecoin is perhaps one of the most unique offerings. It has captivated cryptocurrency enthusiasts since 2014.

Dogecoin (DOGE) is an open-source cryptocurrency that comes from a fork of the Litecoin code base. As the name suggests, it is largely based on the DOGE meme that took the internet by storm in 2013. The original image depicts a Shiba Inu dog, whose inner monologue is shown in comic sans font.

Billy Markus, a programmer from Oregon, initially came up with the idea for a sort of "joke" cryptocurrency. He reasoned that a more lighthearted currency would have a better chance of attracting widespread attention than Bitcoin. At about the same time, Adobe's Jackson Palmer declared that he was "investing in Dogecoin, pretty sure it's the next big thing" in a now-deleted tweet.

Following a bit of encouragement, Palmer went on to create Dogecoin.com. When Markus stumbled upon the website shortly after its launch, he approached Palmer about making it happen and began work on what is now known as Dogecoin. Following the launch, the cryptocurrency quickly spread through social media. Within months, it reached a market capitalization of several million dollars.

The Dogecoin community has earned a reputation for its charitable contributions. It took off as a tipping system on sites like Reddit, where users would send each other small amounts of Dogecoin to reward content creators.

This generous spirit was echoed in its fundraising events, which we'll mention later.

In mid-2020, a viral video on the video-sharing app TikTok created a chain reaction, which caused the price of DOGE to increase significantly. One user asked others to join him in buying Dogecoin, claiming that "everyone would get rich" buying coins and selling them once the price reached $1.00. The hype escalated, causing Dogecoin to trade at more than 2.5 times what it had in the previous weeks. However, the pump was short-lived and prices started to drop drastically afterwards.

Keep in mind that this type of activity could be considered pump and dump. This type of scheme is illegal in traditional markets because of the dangers to investors. Promoters buy large amounts of an asset before generating hype around it, causing others to experience FOMO on the investment.

As a result, the price rises significantly, the "bomb". Then, developers sell their holdings, leading to "dumping":

With such high selling pressure, the price plummets, as subsequent investors are left with huge losses. As always, do your own research on potential investments. Various online platforms and tutorials offer a wealth of resources on trading and economics, which can help you better understand the cryptocurrency markets.

Take a look at how Dogecoin works. Dogecoin is based on a fork of Litecoin (LTC) called Luckycoin. However, notable changes have since been made to the protocol.

### Blockchain

Similar to Bitcoin, Dogecoin uses a blockchain, where blocks are aggregated through Proof-Of-Work (PoW) Proof-Of-Work. Network participants install open source software on their machines so they can act as full nodes. For those unfamiliar with Blockchain technology, this means that each participant maintains a complete copy of the database, in which all transactions are stored.

The system is decentralized because there is no administrator in control. Instead, users send information directly to each other and rely on cryptographic techniques to know whether their peers are acting honestly.

### Mining and supply

In proof-of-work blockchains like Bitcoin, a process called mining is used to create new coins. Participants must prove to the network that they have done a "job," which can be thought of as revealing an answer to a complex puzzle. The puzzle is solved by hashing the information until the user can provide an output that the network will accept as valid. It is not feasible to produce a solution by hand, so users devote electricity and computing power to try to find it. One important difference between Bitcoin and Litecoin is that the latter does not use the SHA-256 hash function for mining. This was an intentional decision: Litecoin, instead, relies on Scrypt, an ASIC-resistant proof-of-work algorithm.

In simple terms, this means that the specially designed machines used to mine Bitcoin could not compete with the normal computers and GPUs that were used to mine Litecoin. In theory, this would result in a more decentralized mining landscape. However, before long, application-specific integrated circuits for Scrypt emerged.

As a derivative of Litecoin, Dogecoin inherited the Scrypt algorithm. However, to avoid any competition and mitigate security risks, Dogecoin developers switched to a merged mining model, meaning that Litecoin miners could earn Dogecoin simultaneously.

Dogecoin mining targets a block time of one minute and yields a block reward of 10,000 DOGE. There is no maximum supply of units and over a hundred billion are already in circulation. Enthusiasts see the removal of any cap as a good option, as it incentivizes spending the coin and prevents early adopters from benefiting disproportionately.

### What can you do with Dogecoin?

Like many other cryptocurrencies, there are several ways to acquire Dogecoin. You can mine it yourself or accept it as payment for goods and services. However, the easiest method is to buy it through a cryptocurrency exchange. Generally, you will first need to buy Bitcoin or another popular currency and then exchange it for DOGE.

Once you have your Dogecoin, you can use it as you would any other cryptocurrency: hold it long-term in a hardware wallet, exchange it for other currencies, trade it for goods, or tip others with it. Bitrefill is perhaps the easiest way to spend, as you can buy gift cards and vouchers for a variety of retailers, for example; or put it to use through investments in a wide range of opportunity platforms that we'll look at in friendly detail later.

Despite being an asset whose existence revolves around an Internet meme, Dogecoin has developed a dedicated community of users. Eight years later, it maintains a market capitalization of billions of US dollars.

It's not entirely clear whether the market values Dogecoin as a novel cryptocurrency, a viable financial asset, or something in between. But few cryptocurrencies have had the impact that the Shiba Inu coin has, if only because of its status as a meme currency.

So let's keep in mind that, back in 2013, Jackson Palmer, a product manager at Adobe Inc.'s Sydney, Australia office, created Dogecoin as a way to satirize the hype surrounding cryptocurrencies at the time. Palmer was described as a "skeptical-analytical" observer of emerging technology, and his early tweets about his new cryptocurrency venture were tongue-in-cheek. But after receiving countless and multiple positive comments on social media in reaction to his posts; he decided to purchase the Dogecoin.com domain.

Meanwhile, in Portland, Oregon, Billy Markus, a software developer at the well-known IBM company, who was eager to create his own digital currency, but was experiencing great difficulty in promoting his efforts, discovered the Dogecoin rumor. Markus approached Palmer for permission, and so together; they built the software behind a real and true Dogecoin.

Markus based the Dogecoin code on Luckycoin, which itself is derived from Litecoin, and initially used a random reward for block mining, although it was changed to a static reward in March 2014. Dogecoin uses Litecoin's scrypt technology and is a Proof-Of-Work coin.

Palmer and Markus finally decided to launch Dogecoin as a new virtual currency on December 6, 2013. Two weeks later, on December 19, the value of Dogecoin rose 300%, perhaps because China banned its banks from investing in cryptocurrencies.

Dogecoin was introduced and marketed as a "fun" version of

Bitcoin with a Shiba Inu (Japanese dog) as its logo. Dogecoin's informal presentation suited the mood of the burgeoning crypto community. Its scrypt technology and unlimited supply were an argument for a faster, more adaptable and consumer-friendly version of Bitcoin.

Dogecoin is an "inflationary coin," whereas cryptocurrencies like Bitcoin are deflationary because there is a limit to the amount of coins that will be created. Every four years, the amount of Bitcoin released into circulation through mining rewards is halved and its inflation rate is halved until all cryptocurrencies are released.

In January 2014, the Dogecoin community made significant donations, highlighted as, for example; $30,000.00 to fund the Jamaican bobsled team's trip to the Sochi Winter Olympics. In March of the same year, the Dogecoin community donated $11,000.00 in Dogecoin to build a well in Kenya and $55,000.00 in Dogecoin to sponsor NASCAR driver Josh Wise and place the logo of this cryptocurrency on his race car.

Dogecoin is the friendliest and most fun cryptocurrency in the entire crypto world, however, Dogecoin lost some of its joy in 2015 when the crypto community, in general, started to become more serious. The first sign that all is not fun and all was not well with the Dogecoin community was the departure of Jackson Palmer, who said that a "toxic community" had grown up around the coin and the money it produced.

In an interview with Bloomberg in San Francisco (California), Jackson Palmer expressed his concern about the huge amounts of money that continue to flow into this cryptocurrency: "Dogecoin started as a joke and it's important to keep it that way. I see Dogecoin as an indicator of how much euphoria there is in the cryptocurrency market, and how many unwise investments are being made. If a coin that has had no development for many years can reach two billion market cap, it says a lot about the current market and you better pay attention."

One member of that toxic community was Alex Green, also

known as Ryan Kennedy, a British citizen who created a Dogecoin exchange called Moolah. Alex Green (his pseudonym) was known in the community as a generous, reportedly mistakenly gave $15,000.00 instead of $1,500.00 to the NASCAR fundraiser.

Green's exchange convinced community members to donate large sums to help fund the creation of his exchange, but it was later discovered that he had used the donations to purchase over $1.5 million in Bitcoin which in turn allowed him to live a lavish lifestyle. On the other hand, Kennedy was convicted in 2016 of multiple counts of rape and sentenced to serve 11 years in prison.

During and after the crypto bubble of 2017 and 2018, Dogecoin's value soared with the rest of the cryptoverse, peaking in late 2017, and fell with the rest of the cryptoverse during 2018. At its peak, Dogecoin was trading for $0.018 and had a market cap of over $2 billion.

In the summer of 2019, Dogecoin experienced another surge in value along with the rest of the crypto market. Dogecoin enthusiasts rejoiced when crypto exchange Binance listed the coin, and many thought Tesla CEO Elon Musk had endorsed the coin in a cryptic tweet.

However, Dogecoin's infrastructure has not been a central source of concern for the coin's developers, who are still volunteers. However, one of the reasons it continues to operate and trade is its active community of miners. As CryptoIQ's Zachary Mashiach rightly puts it, "Numerous Scrypt miners still prefer Dogecoin (DOGE) over other Scrypt PoW cryptocurrencies. In fact, the hash rate of Dogecoin (DOGE) is approximately 150 TH / s. This is just below the Litecoin (LTC) hash rate of 170 TH / s, probably because Dogecoin (DOGE) can be merged with Litecoin (LTC), which means that miners can mine both cryptocurrencies simultaneously using the same job. Essentially and virtually everyone who mines Litecoin (LTC) also chooses to mine Dogecoin (DOGE), because the combined mining of Dogecoin (DOGE) increases profits.

As of December 21, 2020, Dogecoin's market cap ranking was 43, with a market cap of $611 million."

The meme-inspired digital currency, Dogecoin, continues to capture the public's attention today; even more so as none other than Tesla CEO Elon Musk and rapper Snoop Dogg have dedicated time to post a series of tweets referring to the cryptocurrency, which without a doubt; and influencer style has raised the price of the already highly recognized "meme" currency, the Dogecoin.

After this series of tweets, Dogecoin jumped 31% achieving a record value of $0.083745. The digital currency now ranks as one of the top 10 digital currencies by market value, according to CoinMarketCap. In one instance, Musk tweeted an instructional YouTube video about Dogecoin, while Snoop Dogg uploaded a photo of the dog that inspired Dogecoin with the caption "@elonmusk."

Musk has been actively tweeting about the coin since its GameStop knockoff spike. In January, Dogecoin surged more than 600%, fueled by Reddit mania surrounding GameStop.

Dogecoin started in 2013 as a joke between two engineers. IBM software engineer Billy Markus and Adobe software engineer Jackson Palmer. A professional duo who hadn't even met when they successfully combined two of the biggest phenomena of 2013: Bitcoin and "DOGE". The result: Dogecoin.

Dogecoin was a product that people started using as soon as it was launched, immediately, to the surprise of the two engineers. More than one million unique visitors came to Dogecoin.com during the website's first month.

The dux meme that gained popularity in 2013 featured an image of a Shiba Inu dog with Comic Sans thought bubbles coming out of it with almost monosyllabic ideas. The meme could be used to express anything from jokes about naps, early mornings, diets, even space exploration.

Dogecoin has its own "friendly and funny" mascot, it is DOGE; a Japanese Shiba Inu hunting dog, which became a trend from Japan, after kindergarten teacher Atsuko Sato published in 2010 a picture with her dog Kabosu, becoming very popular in several social networks, but thanks to Reddit and its multiple publications which gave it an unexpected level, becoming over time one of the most notorious images and memes on the network. It is the face of a Shiba Inu that looks sideways at the camera and has around him a series of phrases written incorrectly. Kabosu's face began to appear in different and varied objects; memes of all kinds. It was not until 2013, when the face of this now famous canine appeared for the first time on a cryptocurrency, at the initiative of Palmer and Markus.

Before the product was launched, Palmer, who had been following developments in the cryptocurrency world, absentmindedly tweeted, "Invest in Dogecoin, pretty sure it's the next big thing."

He received a few responses encouraging him to pursue the idea, and a week later he bought the Dogecoin.com domain. Inevitably, the idea was picked up on Reddit, a hotbed of dux activity in 2013.

Meanwhile, in Portland, Billy Markus had been trying to program his own digital currency that would appeal to a broader demographic than the speculators who have flooded Bitcoin since the currency launched in 2008. But the project had gone nowhere. Then he stumbled upon Dogecoin.com within a day or two after the site went live.

"The first thing I said was, 'This is so much fun.' Then I said, 'I should do this coin,'" Markus said in 2013.

Markus tweeted Palmer saying he wanted in on the venture, and before Palmer responded, he began reconfiguring the publicly available Bitcoin source code to convert its user-oriented elements into the dux meme.

Finally, and in the month of December 2013, Palmer responded and the partnership was formed. A little over a week after Palmer's joke tweet, Dogecoin was released.

The currency was derived from the open source software project, Litecoin. Unlike Bitcoin. Dogecoin does not have a limit on the amount of coins that can be produced in the system.

Dogecoin has its own "friendly and funny" mascot, DOGE; a

Japanese Shiba Inu hunting dog, which became a trend from Japan after kindergarten teacher Atsuko Sato posted a picture with her dog Kabosu in 2010, becoming very popular in several social networks.

But thanks to Reddit and its multiple publications that gave it an unexpected level, becoming over time one of the most notorious images and memes on the network. It is the face of a Shiba Inu that looks sideways at the camera and has around him a series of phrases written incorrectly.

Kabosu's face began to appear in different and varied objects; memes of all kinds. It was not until 2013, when the face of this canine appeared for the first time on a cryptocurrency, at the initiative of Palmer and Markus.

The digital currency instantly exploded on Reddit, generating a market value of $8 million at the time. It was made popular by the Internet practice of "tipping," which was a way to reward people on the web for doing "good deeds," such as sharing an idea or making a platform more accessible.

Just a week after launch, Dogecoin became the second most tipped currency, its creators said.

The digital currency has long contributed to a culture distinguished by a kind of irreverence for institutions like Wall Street. Not surprisingly, Reddit users buy shares alongside GameStop and AMC in trading against large hedge funds.

Dogecoin developed its own culture in 2013, largely because the coin has a lower barrier to entry than Bitcoin for people who might be interested in cryptocurrencies.

Dogecoin is the most popular and peculiar cryptocurrency on the planet. The total value of Dogecoin in circulation is over USD 53 billion, which is not bad for a digital currency that started as a simple joke.

Like all cryptocurrencies, Dogecoin is a digital currency that can be bought and sold as an investment and spent as money.

Although each crypto is unique, Dogecoin shares some similarities with its better-known peers - its code is based on the Litecoin script, for example. But it has a couple of key differences. Unlike Bitcoin, which has pegged the number of coins available in the market at 21 million, Dogecoin already has more than 129 billion coins in circulation and will continue to make new blocks of coins available for mining every year. That's part of the reason why one Dogecoin is currently valued at just under 40 cents on the dollar and one Bitcoin is worth about $35,910.00 (June 13, 2021)

Dogecoin is no longer the fun joke of its early days. Its popularity has skyrocketed astronomically this year, in part because of the widespread adoption of Bitcoin and other cryptocurrencies.

Tesla's renowned CEO, Elon Musk, is the most notorious and prominent supporter of Dogecoin. A simple tweet to his more than 50 million followers can make the cryptocurrency skyrocket in a fraction of seconds. Something that already happened last April 15, 2021, when Musk tweeted, "DOGE barking at the moon" and shared a photo of a painting by Spanish artist Joan Miro, which is titled "Dog barking at the moon."

Dogecoin has also enjoyed something of a cult status on Reddit, where a popular group, not unlike the WallStreetBets group behind the GameStop rally, decided earlier this year to push its value "to the moon." Dogecoin soared more than 600% as a result.

Whether or not it's a smart investment remains a question. Bitcoin, which is more actively traded and more widely accepted, is subject to extreme volatility, so Dogecoin could also crumble without warning. But its rise this year has certainly been impressive.

Who hasn't benefited from the coin's breakneck growth is Markus, who sold all of his Dogecoin when he was laid off in 2015. He used the money to buy a Honda Civic.

At present, Dogecoin is part of the Top 10 of the world's top cryptocurrencies, ranking #6, at a value of $0.31 and a market capitalization of $40,325,774,653 Dogecoin has been gradually growing with shocking peaks for the market and the crypto ecosystem. There are those who attribute its impressive growth and Dogecoin's most recent takeoff to the publications made by Tesla CEO Elon Musk on his official Twitter account, who through his company has invested $1.5 billion in Bitcoin, announcing the acceptance of payments in said cryptocurrency as the main form for its Tesla electric cars; he has referred to Dogecoin as his favorite currency and "the people's currency". However, there are many crypto investors who warn that such statements should not be taken seriously.

At first glance and right off the bat, Dogecoin is without a doubt and has become the most fun and friendly cryptocurrency in the entire crypto universe. Dogecoin has its own exclusive difference that makes it particularly unique among all the others, thanks to a fantastic and incredible community, made up of people who like each other and enjoy what they do, especially; being part of this active virtual family.

Dogecoin is loved by the Z generation, by animal lovers; and most especially by those who love and care for dogs, not to mention those who are amused and inspired by memes. Dogecoin, without knowing it; made a powerful incursion into the personal subjectivity of a large community.

In the growing world of cryptocurrencies and their unbridled expansion within the digital ecosystem, we have seen emerge and disappear, under various circumstances; any number of digital currencies that have estimated in this space an opportunity of interest in the cryptoactive field. Today there are more than 10,000 cryptocurrencies, standing firm in the face of market fluctuation and about 800 have died or disappeared.

636 were part of solid crypto projects, but failed to materialize, 125 were outright hoaxes, 55 were born as a simple prank and 12 were hacked. However, the tendency to remain an active presence is in the secrecy of their targets. For example, in the darkest time or very bad reputation that adorned the existence of Bitcoin, for being involved in large and important black market transactions on the Dark Web, Dogecoin appears as an alternative that had nothing to do with shady affairs, relationships and exchanges.

Dogecoin refreshed the environment with sympathy, with new

and fresh airs that generated from the first instant; a certain level of joy after a meme that coined in its image. A wonderful objective brings Dogecoin to light, to fan the market, generate tranquility and create confidence that there are more positive projects that seek to be based on respect and honesty; knowing that anything can happen and understanding; how he lived it, that from good also comes ambition and evil, but that they manage to overcome.

Memes and Cryptocurrencies:

Dogecoin Situation: A patient is waiting to receive his first dose of the anti-covid-19 vaccine and it comes with a special dose of cryptocurrency advice. The nurse administering the vaccine comments, "-I'm buying Dogecoin, the canine-inspired meme coin. Its price varies wildly in part due to Elon Musk's tweets and the public reaction from his community." Vaccine placed, the patient receives a recommendation, in this pandemic era. "Remember, I bought some Dogecoin."

We are in the era of investing by memes. Some people are throwing tons and tons of money at a stock or a currency, not because they believe there is something significantly different about the underlying value of the asset, but because it became popular on the Internet and they think it's fun, cool or just something different to do. Many of them buy into the hype generated on platforms like Reddit and TikTok and join. Crypto is the compendium of all this, as well as all the mess and confusion that comes with it.

" Some things are clearly legitimate and some things are clearly lies, and there's also a long list of things that are a little more confusing," said Sam Bankman-Fried, director of Alameda Research and cryptocurrency derivatives exchange FTX. "In this financial environment, sometimes just a token with a meme or a stock with a meme or an asset with a meme is enough to get you a $20 billion.oo million valuation."

You may be familiar with the GameStop saga earlier this year, when an army of traders on WallStreetBets helped fuel a dramatic rise in the retailer's stock price seemingly out of nowhere. They managed to upset some big names on Wall Street. There are some investors who will say they were in the GameStop trade because they believe in the value of the startup, but many of them were there for GameStop as a meme.

But cryptocurrencies have been trading like this pretty much since the beginning. The meme aspect has always been part of the appeal. Bitcoin, Dogecoin and Ethereum are as much a cultural and Internet phenomenon as they are technological or financial. And as cryptocurrencies go mainstream, so do memes, especially as people are getting into day trading without much of an investment plan.

Although cryptocurrencies have been around for more than a decade, they are capturing more headlines recently. The price of Bitcoin, the original cryptocurrency, has gone from $5,000 to $6,000 a year ago to over $60,000 for some time. Both institutional and ordinary investors have agreed.

But cryptocurrencies are also incredibly volatile, as evidenced by the wild fluctuations seen at certain and certain times. A sudden transaction on May 19, 2021, caused the price of Bitcoin to drop 30 percent, and hundreds of thousands of traders were liquidated entirely. Some other "altcoins," i.e., anything other than Bitcoin; also plunged.

Some cryptocurrency traders say they have laser-sighted eyes, meaning they don't deviate from Bitcoin's course at all. But for many new investors, it's been a crash course in crypto chaos. That's when the meme meets reality.

"People who aren't plugged into this cryptocurrency thing 24/7 should definitely be a lot more careful than a lot of people advocate being," said Sam Trabucco, a cryptocurrency trader at Alameda Research, a specialized quantitative trading firm; referring to those who dabble in the meme fever.

In the current furor, some of what is going on seems a bit mocking and even nefarious. Ethan Allen's stock price has risen because people are confusing its ticker symbol, ETH, with Ethereum. Dave Portnoy, the founder of Barstool Sports, has said he is investing in a coin that could be a Ponzi scheme.

And according to an FTC report, consumers have lost more than $80 million to crypto scams in the past six months alone, including $2 million to Musk impersonators alone. Many politicians and regulators are calling for stricter rules around the space. It is easy to imitate a meme and adopt the persona of a celebrity with fraudulent and criminal intentions.

"Yes, there is an opportunity," said Ed Moya, Senior Market Analyst at OANDA, "but I feel the risk is greater than anything we've seen on Wall Street."

Bitcoin has gone through boom and bust cycles before, and pump-and-dump schemes in smaller coins right now are everywhere. In a meme economy, you may feel like you're in on the crypto joke, but the joke may still be on you. And memes go in and out of fashion.

For one thing, while GameStop's stock hasn't fallen to its pre-memefication value, it's still trading well below its frenzied highs. Musk may find Bitcoin and Dogecoin interesting and fun right now, but he probably won't do it forever, he has already changed his mind more than once. Many normal people went into trading during the pandemic, including crypto trading, because they are bored at home. Now that life is gradually returning to normal, scanning random sub reddits to rally behind a new coin, funny image or meme might fall further down the priority list.

Remember the situation with the patient and the nurse? When he came back for his second dose of covid-19, he decided not to ask the nurse anything about his investment in Dogecoin, the doggy virtual currency. I just remembered that he was trying to accumulate 1,000 Dogecoin before this one hit $1,00 and knew he probably still had plenty of time to get there.

We have arrived and are already entering the era of investment memes There are tons of people who are trading cryptocurrencies for substantive reasons. But much of the crypto frenzy seems recently driven by, not that. Some friend of yours or mine, maybe the high school classmate isn't trying to buy a Shiba Inu coin because he thinks it's the technology of the future.

In the case of Bitcoin, its technology is a really important part of the meme. Dogecoin, it's, "Let's extract all of that and just focus on the meme," said Galen Moore, director of data and indices at Coin-Desk. Probably the most appropriate question you have to ask yourself is how long do you think that meme can last?

Some dedicated traders say they intend to "hold" or have "diamond hands," meaning they won't let go no matter what. When the going gets tough, there is a core group determined to meme through them. The joke is still funny, even if the financial situation is not.

It's no coincidence that there is a proliferation of "dirty coins" and meme coins, two terms that are sometimes synonymous with altcoins; they often skyrocket and collapse quickly. "It's really easy for someone on TikTok or whatever to just copy or release a token with a funny name, and then you get into meme trading," said Neeraj Agrawal, head of communications at Coin Center, a crypto policy think tank.

Pump-and-dump schemes, where a group of people increase the price of a cryptocurrency to create a buying furor, increase the price and then sell, are common. They are a way of trying to weaponize the meme. Even if you go into a pump-and-dump scheme with your eyes wide open, you may not realize that you are actually the one who is out of the scheme.

"If you buy something called an asscoin, that's up to you," Agrawal said. The ASScoin, or, rather, the Australian Safe Shepherd coin, is real, it exists, and it's also a joke.

The irrational exuberance is now reminiscent of 2017. Back then, there was a proliferation of initial coin offerings (ICOs), with startups offering digital tokens to raise money. They generated a lot of buzz, and some even came with celebrity endorsements. Many of them turned out to be scams, unfortunately.

"We're starting to see the kind of nonsense we've already seen," Agrawal added. "As far as what that means, who knows."

A giant number of people live with the desire, the drive and the relentless get-rich-quick mentality.

A combination of things that has contributed to cryptocurrencies' latest takeoff. Some big institutional names started backing Bitcoin. They include billionaire hedge funder Paul Tudor Jones, who said he sees it as an inflation hedge and a "great speculation," and Bank of New York Mellon, the nation's oldest bank, which has announced it will offer Bitcoin services. Musk's interest contributed to the excitement.

Cryptocurrency trading platform Coinbase also went public, solidifying a place in more traditional finance. Cash App and PayPal and Venmo have started accepting some cryptocurrencies; Tesla said it would accept Bitcoins, but then changed course. But overall, more people have gotten into cryptocurrencies in recent months and years because it was easier to do so.

"The received wisdom is that the fourth quarter was institution-driven and the first quarter was retail-driven," said CoinDesk's Moore. The excitement around cryptocurrencies, some of it financial, some of it meme-inspired, generated more enthusiasm. Bitcoin is the best-performing asset of the last decade, and it's hard for both pros and newbies not to look at that and think, why not try to get in?

A lot of what has driven this market has been this relentless get-rich-quick mentality. There have been several altcoins where you'll see this coin go up 30 percent on some random day, and people were buying these coins blindly.

There are thousands of cryptocurrencies and creating a new one is really easy. Some of the options are quite serious projects, although there are many smart people who would say absolutely nothing about this; others are a joke. Even the price of a cryptocurrency at any given time can be debatable.

In crypto, there are 20 major exchanges and there are no laws regulating that prices have to be similar across exchanges, so what the price of Bitcoin is is more confusing than in traditional finance."

In the relatively short life of cryptocurrencies, there have been multiple rounds of booms and busts, most notably in 2013 and 2017. The last time this happened, about four years ago, Bitcoin's price reached nearly $20,000 before falling back to $3,000. The decline in certain seasons has led to speculation that this is the beginning of the end of the latest cryptocurrency boom cycle. There is more institutional acceptance this time around, which some people in the space say they believe means this time will be different. Of course, institutions can always leave and many investors are easily spooked. Volatility is actually a feature, not a bug. It's part of how this system works.

There is also a learning curve to getting into cryptocurrencies, not only when it comes to understanding volatility, but also when it comes to avoiding getting scammed or losing your coins. The amount of money people have lost in crypto scams increased 1,000 percent in the last six months compared to the same period last year. When cryptocurrencies go missing, it is often difficult, if not impossible, to trace them, which is why it has sometimes been a method of choice for crime and money laundering. There have been multiple high-profile hacks, and sometimes people simply lose their cryptocurrency because they forget a password or lose their keys. It is estimated that approximately $140 billion worth of Bitcoins are lost.

Novelties come and go, changes and restructurings, but there are still many regulatory questions. The whole meme-driven retail trading trend has prompted calls from politicians and regulators for stricter rules. The same is true for cryptocurrencies. But no agency is even the clear regulator of cryptocurrencies. The Securities and Exchange Commission (SEC), the Commodities Futures Trading Commission (CFTC) and the Treasury Department's Financial Crimes Enforcement Network (FinCEN) all intervene in some capacity. Cryptocurrencies are generally considered a commodity, like oil or gold, and not a security, like a stock, or a currency, like the dollar. That contributes to confusion about who is in charge.

The IRS also has to deal with the tax component. The IRS recently released a plan that would include requiring crypto transactions over $10,000 to be reported, as is the case with cash. This new policy aims to undermine some of the appeal of cryptocurrencies, where transactions often go unnoticed.

The lack of regulation, in many ways, makes the meme element more potent. If there seem to be no rules, why not create an ASS dollar coin, hype it up, and then cheat people out of thousands of dollars?

SEC Chairman Gary Gensler has said he would like to see a tighter regulatory framework around cryptocurrencies. "This is a fairly volatile, you could say highly volatile, asset class, and the investing public would benefit from greater investor protection on crypto exchanges." But it's something that would have to be addressed in Congress. There are some proposed federal legislation related to cryptocurrencies, but it's unclear what their prospects are: lawmakers tend not to be good at figuring out the technology.

However, it is not necessarily the case that there are absolutely no rules around cryptocurrencies. A crime is still a crime and money laundering is illegal regardless of the currency. In 2019, researcher Chainalysis tracked $2.8 billion in Bitcoins that went from criminal activity to crypto exchanges. But many of the rules around the space right now are not cryptocurrency-specific.

There are robust regulatory regimes in place for U.S.-regulated service providers in the crypto space. The problem is that regulation, for the most part, is being repurposed to apply to a technology where some of those regulations are not a perfect fit.

It's not just what the U.S. does that matters; it's other countries as well. After all, the goal of projects like Bitcoin is to be global. Some other countries have more lax rules than the U.S. But as we've seen recently, international regulatory threats can also cause price changes.

China recently took action and thus triggered drastic actions against crypto transactions and shut down crypto mining operations there, which caused the May 19, 2021 drop in crypto prices. Hong Kong has proposed requiring exchanges there to be licensed by its markets regulator and limiting cryptocurrency trading to professionals, a big problem given that many of the world's largest exchanges are located there. Given the environmental impact of cryptocurrency mining, some people would like to see it regulated and gone forever.

Of course, many of the people who have piled into cryptocurrency trading in recent months are not interested in the regulatory regime surrounding the emerging technology, nor are they dedicated to the long-term project. They jumped on a meme coin and went for a ride, many of them learning that making a quick buck on something they saw trending on the Internet is easier said than done.

Some people will make a lot of money; more people will lose a lot of money, but hopefully something good will come out of all of this. At the very least, they'll get the memes they met along the way.

# TWO

# IN-DEPTH UNDERSTANDING OF DOGECOIN AND ITS DEVELOPMENT

Prominent investors and experts in cryptocurrencies, involved in various projects, know Dogecoin very well and closely, since 2013. Many of them agree that, in the early days of the coin, between 2013 and 2014, they joined this community and participated some of them as developers. It will never cease to be said that Dogecoin was a joke or a parody that tried to cause laughter in those who were very serious about cryptocurrencies. Something that definitely caught on very well.

The people who continued to be part of the large Dogecoin community, which no longer includes its creator and founder, Billy Markus, who abandoned his wonderful project in 2015, partly maintained their plan so that it would not die completely, but their support turned out to be so residual that even their technology was not subjected to updates. Now, they are currently trying to fix it. Dogecoin is a fork of Litecoin, which is also a fork of Bitcoin.

Working with its own Blockchain, which in recent years has not been subjected to technological updates based on current standards, it generates endless difficulties of synchronization and operation with wallets. This could mean that, if you move Dogecoin, you may end up losing some money due to problems in the platform. Now, with the unleashed "DOGE fever", many developers are back and are making changes to make the system work and thus be able to catch up, taking advantage of the opportunity that many could also produce large funds.

Dogecoin's problems do not stop there. It can be easily mined, but it is expensive to do it at home, there is no shortage because about five million dollars worth of coins enter the market every day, there is no mining limit, offering a single great positive point: it is a coin.

THE MOST INTERESTING thing is that she exists, that you can safely send and receive money in the form of Dogecoin, that is, like the rest or most cryptocurrencies, but of course, it has nothing else. There is no beyond in this project with certain ideas for the future or some certain strategy to maintain the project.

TO ALL THIS, many experts add a key determinant point that has also been mentioned even by Elon Musk, and that is the concentration of money. Only a few investors accumulate most of the Dogecoin on the market. The number one or head in the crypto ranking, has about 28% of the total existing money in circulation.

Although it is not known precisely who it is, there is speculation that behind this fortune could be the Robinhood App. Fortunately, this is something that does not affect the price at all at first, because there is no established limit in coins, but it does depend on one of these rich whales in Dogecoin not to sell. If, right off the bat, it sought to get rid of a good part of them, the price would plummet, or something like going into free fall.

Well-known developers are quite critical of the rise of Dogecoin, even daring to point out that its success could be clouded and murky, which would be very serious for the crypto industry that has made so many efforts to be taken seriously. This is a situation that would affect the industry more than anything else, because it makes it look like a volatile place where successes and achievements only depend on the money people invest, which can be easily manipulated and there is nothing else.

Can Dogecoin sustain something like this over time? Ultimately, one thing is certain. We do not know, nor are we aware of how long this success will last.

Today, it would seem that this would depend a lot on Elon Musk and the rest of the people who follow and support him for the hype and the bet. But as soon as that happens, would it take a nosedive and a lot of people would be left in the lurch?

MANY HAVE WONDERED how it is possible that Elon Musk sees so much potential in a cryptocurrency that started and took its first steps inspired by a joke, that runs on the most basic open source code and that has enjoyed virtually no recent development on GitHub. Critics and experts in the field point to the GitHub page as sterile and wonder if there is at least one real developer for Dogecoin.

TO THIS SITUATION, the response from Ross Nicoll, software engineer and part-time programmer at Dogecoin, is that he sees no point in "expending development effort just to expend development effort," especially when updates applied to Dogecoin can take up to

18 months to be adopted by the entire network. So, "Why would we do a more frequent update? It seemed crazy."

NICOLL DECIDED to join the cryptocurrency world and industry after spending 10 years in academia, excelling as a researcher focused on application design and development. Most recently, Nicoll was in charge of leading the technical development of Smart Contracts for the R3 Enterprise Blockchain project, working closely with commercial banks. Ross Nicoll also served for a short time, in his innovative work within the renowned NFT CryptoKitties project.

HIS VERY GROUNDED APPROACH; reflects his extensive experience in commercial Blockchain development, where proceeding to release a new update every three or four months a year, as some other Blockchain projects tend to do, would prove excessive.

"We are not trying to absorb massive amounts of money by making millionaires or billionaires out of developers" and neither "are we trying to reinvent technology that other 3000 Blockchains have already reinvented" - Ross Nicoll.

BITCOIN'S own model is closely followed by Dogecoin, but, like Litecoin, this cryptocurrency uses a different code, Scrypt; which consumes less energy and is much more aligned to the new ecological stance suggested by Elon Musk regarding cryptocurrencies.

For Nicoll, the crypto network currently suffers from "performance issues with the network's own synchronization," this is something that could be solved with an upcoming update, thoroughly designed to act as a proper foundation for many of the radical changes to come, some of which have been endorsed by Musk.

. . .

AS THE DOGECOIN market raises its temperature, Nicoll; part-time developer has acknowledged that interest in generating development for the coin has skyrocketed. "We're seeing a flood of developers jumping in to work on it." There is another group of developers who have dubbed themselves "mainstream," such as a team in New York that has recently emerged. Which excites Ross Nicoll, who has expressed his honest wishes to see more development teams that are dedicated to doing every day, more new things for the cryptoverse. Those who have worked on Dogecoin so far, have mostly been engaged in part time work on a part time basis.

With great satisfaction Ross has dedicated himself to act as a developer for Dogecoin, with the complacency of working and planning his strategies from the comfort of his home, at ease and with abnegation; investing only part time or half time for a virtual currency that has been awakening interest, empathy and gaining followers who yearn to see Dogecoin every day in better and outstanding positions.

THE STRUCTURE OF DOGECOIN, its conformation, configuration and development; do not require a Senior Technical Leader, this digital currency has the privilege of having Ross Nicoll as a part-time developer and great follower like Elon Musk; who have managed to impact the Dogecoin market, effectively and strategically gaining and expanding more and more space on the network.

Nicoll tends to question how projects can claim to become fully decentralized even when they rely on a large handful of frontline contributors. In Dogecoin you would like to have 100, 200 or 1,000 second-tier contributors, sheltered by three or four core contributors: that's decentralized. Dogecoin is looked at as if its community is out of reason, but it's something that makes sense to Nicoll.

With such a goal in mind, Nicoll has dedicated himself to broadcasting his coding directly via Twitch in order to train and educate the next generation of developers in favor of Dogecoin. One of his most fervent wishes is for current and new developers to work on projects such as the long-awaited DOGEthereum bridge, and decentralized finance (DeFi) projects to introduce smart contract support into DOGE.

THANKS to the good price DOGE enjoys, DOGE today has sufficient funds in its "petty cash". The current core development team is constantly establishing a framework and guidance on how these funds will be used, given their size. After turning down money from Musk and other large potential investors, which Nicoll chose not to mention in order to avoid being beholden to one person, they see no point in continuing to raise more and more funds until they have a clear and concrete plan for how the money will be used.

ON ONE OCCASION ROSS NICOLL, the developer of Dogecoin stated that Elon Musk has been since 2019, advising the small team working for this cryptocurrency, likewise Musk has offered to fund Dogecoin with the desire to see it become the most dominant crypto on the market. However, inspired by his confidence and powers; Nicoll and his other developers have taken pains to lay the groundwork for the bigger and better upgrade that Dogecoin deserves.

Any number of Dogecoin followers see Elon Musk, the biggest cryptocurrency influencer from the social network Twitter, as a kind of honorary developer and booster. Musk once tweeted about Nicoll and the three other lead developers with responsibility for the Dogecoin Blockchain, saying, "Working with DOGE developers to improve efficiency of system transactions. Potentially promising." May 13, 2021.

This tweet got Dogecoiners and certainly Nicoll himself very excited, who considered these developments as a typical surreal episode in the best style of the sci-fi series "Black Mirror". Since Musk met Dogecoin, he has shown his enthusiasm for this virtual currency and his desire to see it become the most widely used in the world.

TO DATE, technologist Elon Musk's involvement in Dogecoin, the cryptocurrency that took its first steps as a replica to Bitcoin, had been a secret, even though his tweets have made Dogecoin soar by up to 10,000% since the beginning of 2021.

MUSK FIRST TWEETED about the project in 2019, when he was offered, and accepted; the title of honorary CEO for Dogecoin in the eye of the storm, in the face of a community that had languished in large numbers after the token's founders had abandoned it in 2015. Since then, there have been five developers - Ross Nicoll, Michi Lumin, Max Keller, Patrick Lodder and "Sporklin", who sadly passed away from cancer in April this year, have dedicated some of their time to work on the open source Dogecoin project in their spare time and dealings. It can be said that this team doesn't really work; they are dedicated to doing something that unites them, that they are passionate about and that they enjoy.

Elon Musk, an active member on the social network Twitter, sends targeted messages from time to time with mention of Dogecoin, and every time this happens, the developers of the coin enter into a turbulent activity or what is the same, a "flurry of activity"; product of the effect generated by the comments or opinions that Musk, in jest or total seriousness, makes about Dogecoin.

DOGECOIN IS a cryptocurrency that runs under Blockchain tech-nology, similarly to Bitcoin and Ethereum. Blockchain is a secure distributed digital ledger that stores all transactions made with a decentralized digital currency.

.  .  .

ALL HOLDERS CARRY an identical copy of the Dogecoin blockchain ledger, which is frequently updated with all new transactions in the cryptocurrency. Like other cryptocurrencies, the Dogecoin Blockchain network uses cryptography to keep all transactions secure.

PEOPLE CALLED miners use computers to solve complex mathematical equations in order to process transactions and record them on the Dogecoin blockchain, a system called proof-of-work PoW (Proof-Of-Work). In exchange for processing transactions and backing up the Blockchain ledger, miners get additional Dogecoin, which they can then hold or sell on the open market.

DOGECOIN CAN BE USED for payments and purchases, but it is not a very effective store of value. This is mainly because there is no lifetime limit on the amount of Dogecoins that can be created by mining, which means that the cryptocurrency is highly inflationary, by design. The blockchain rewards miners for their work by creating millions of new Dogecoins every day, making it difficult for speculative price gains in Dogecoin to sustain over time.

To reiterate, Dogecoin is a cryptocurrency that is based on the code of Bitcoin, the world's number one cryptocurrency. DOGE, which as we have already seen; was born as a fork of Luckycoin, which, in turn, was a fork of Litecoin.

DOGECOIN'S CONSENSUS mechanism is based on Litecoin's Scrypt. For this reason, DOGE buys many of its own functionalities with Bitcoin. As in Bitcoin, the participants and members of the DOGE blockchain network protect the network and the creation of blocks by verifying transactions. The difference of DOGE is that it has a particular much lighter architecture, which allows it to process transactions faster than Bitcoin. For each block generated by miners, they get 10,000 DOGE.

The founders and creators of this cryptocurrency designed the Internet's favorite currency par excellence with a maximum limit of up to 100 billion DOGE. However, the team decided at a certain point, to remove the limit a couple of months after its launch. This is one of the reasons why its price does not tend to increase as much as it does with other cryptocurrencies.

CURRENTLY, DOGE has an inflationary supply, generating 5 billion new DOGE each year.

With its price over 12,000% this year, and with big names, such as Elon Musk talking and tweeting about it, Dogecoin has become one of the most popular cryptocurrencies, along with Bitcoin, which itself hit a new record high of over $63,000,00 Searches like "Is Dogecoin the next Bitcoin?" are even trending on Google and social media. But the two cryptocurrencies have big and very marked differences between them. Here are three important distinctions between Dogecoin and Bitcoin, according to experts and insiders in the cryptoverse.

BITCOIN HAS BUILT-IN scarcity "There are many differences between Dogecoin and Bitcoin," in the estimation of Meltem Demirors, chief strategy officer at CoinShares.

One of the "most important" is the supply of each.

Dogecoin is inflationary, meaning more DOGE is printed every minute of every day, something that gives DOGE a potentially infinite supply.

For example, "every minute of every day, 10,000 more Dogecoin are issued. That equates to nearly 15 million DOGE per day or more than 5 billion DOGE per year.

.  .  .

AN UNLIMITED SUPPLY condition can negatively affect the value over time.

Bitcoin, on the other hand, has a finite supply of 21 million, which creates a built-in scarcity, similar to the way gold or diamonds are valuable because they are scarce.

THIS SCARCITY IS the fundamental reason Bitcoin bulls advocate holding the cryptocurrency for the long term, because it is limited, as demand increases, so should the price of Bitcoin.

BECAUSE OF THIS DIFFERENCE, you see a large number of people trading Dogecoin in the short term, with investors hoping to make a quick profit and choosing to hold Bitcoin for much longer.

DOGECOIN WAS CREATED **as a joke**

ANOTHER DIFFERENCE between Dogecoin and Bitcoin is the premise upon which each was created. Bitcoin was launched in 2009 with an extremely detailed white paper written by Satoshi Nakamoto, the pseudonym used by the creator(s) of Bitcoin. Nakamoto's intention was for Bitcoin to become a prominent decentralized digital currency. Bitcoin supporters see the cryptocurrency as digital gold and a hedge against inflation.

CONFIDENCE IN BITCOIN has grown with institutional and retail investors during its 12-year run, which has allowed the cryptocurrency to reach insurmountable record prices in recent months. In comparison, Dogecoin was created as a joke in 2013 by software engineers Billy Markus and Jackson Palmer. Based on the DOGE meme, which portrays a Shiba Inu dog. Markus and Palmer did not intend for Dogecoin to be taken seriously and become what it is today.

DOGECOIN WAS CREATED AS A JOKE, Markus wrote in a post to Reddit. "I threw it all together, without any expectations or plan. It took me about 3 hours to make."

As a result and without a doubt, Dogecoin lacks technical development and is not as secure as Bitcoin.

OVER THE YEARS, Markus was surprised to see how quickly the Dogecoin community grew, as it was joined by a common love for the Shiba Inu dog meme, and recently, the cryptocurrency exploded after social media buzz from the likes of Musk and Mark Cuban.

"Dogecoin currently exists as a kind of inside joke," says Ledbetter.

BUT FOR MANY PEOPLE, investing is becoming a form of entertainment. For Dogecoin, the meme is the message. As the influence of FinTwit, Twitter of the financial industry grows; so will memes and the way they move our markets.

HOWEVER, both Dogecoin and Bitcoin have been called risky investments, as cryptocurrencies are highly volatile. In fact, experts warn that investors proceed with caution before buying Dogecoin, as they consider its rally to be highly speculative. In turn, experts warn that people should only invest what they can afford to lose.

. . .

BITCOIN HAS A WELL-FUNDED ecosystem Although for many years Dogecoin was developed by engineers who copied the exact code of Bitcoin's software, Bitcoin has an extensive and well-funded ecosystem that does not exist with Dogecoin.

MIKE NOVOGRATZ, all-around crypto crack and CEO of Galaxy Digital, told CNBC's "Squawk Box" on April 20, 2021, that Bitcoin is "a well-thought-out, distributed store of value that has lasted 12 years and is growing in adoption, where Dogecoin literally has two guys who own 30% of the entire supply."

NOVOGRATZ WAS CONCERNED at the thought that once it ramps up and boosts enthusiasm, there will be no developers on it and no institutions entering its community.

As he moves forward with his investment strategy, it is vital to better understand the differences between Bitcoin and Dogecoin. Bitcoin, as the world's first cryptocurrency, set the pace for what is now a financial revolution. The impact of this currency on the world cannot be underestimated. Since its inception, it has helped inspire other exciting and interesting projects in the market. One such project is Dogecoin.

## Bitcoin vs Dogecoin

WHEN SATOSHI NAKAMOTO published the Bitcoin white paper 12 years ago, it was the first time a viable digital currency was created. Unlike his predecessors, Bitcoin's anonymous creator was able to overcome the problem of double-spending that had plagued previous attempts to create a digital currency.

Double-spending is a term that refers to a hacking strategy in which an individual will make a payment and, before the payment is processed, forward the same coins to another party. Clearly, being able to send the same coins to different people would crash any monetary system. Nakamoto overcame this problem by integrating a timestamp within the hash algorithm.

Nakamoto realized that, if the timestamp became part of the hash algorithm, it would be impossible for the same coins to be spent twice because they would have to be sent at exactly the same time. This discovery was revolutionary and is what allowed Bitcoin to become the world's first true cryptocurrency.

## DEVELOPMENT OF DOGECOIN

THE DEVELOPMENT of Dogecoin was largely based on the sound principles that Bitcoin introduced to the market. The coin's founders, Billy Markus and Jackson Palmer, were very familiar with Bitcoin and how it leveraged Blockchain technology to accomplish its tasks. Both Dogecoin founders had backgrounds in computing. Markus was a software engineer at IBM and Palmer worked for Adobe as a programmer.

Their experience helped them create Dogecoin with little effort. Surprisingly, Markus has claimed that it took less than 3 hours to fully program Dogecoin. He explained that he went through the Bitcoin coding and simply removed any place that said Bitcoin and added Dogecoin. As a result, Dogecoin is almost a direct replica on Bitcoin in many ways. Dogecoin entered the market on December 6, 2013.

DESPITE THEIR TECHNICAL SIMILARITIES, these two projects entered the market for two very different purposes. Bitcoin was created to provide the world with a viable alternative to the current financial system. The coding and technical document of the currency are full of indicators of this purpose. For example, the first block in the Bitcoin blockchain, also called the Genesis Block, has the words "The Times 03 / Jan / 2009 Chancellor on the verge of the second bailout for banks" embedded in it.

THIS SECRET MESSAGE speaks to the true intent of this currency. The message was a reference to the Times headline at the time. Nakamoto realized that the world was beholden to a financial system that had less to do with prosperity and instead focused on maintaining control over the population through currency manipulation. The central banking system had once again decided to alter market indicators and measures in an effort to promote manipulation.

It is this mission that helped Bitcoin gain such a staunch following. Many of Bitcoin's most ardent supporters truly believe that Bitcoin is the only way for the masses to break out of this endless cycle of monetary terrorism. They back the currency, not because of its technical prowess, as there are now many more capable currencies that offer a lot of new features and are more scalable. They support the world's first cryptocurrency because they truly believe in Nakamoto's mission to save the world from a future beholden to the world's current central banking system that can print fiat currency whenever it sees fit.

Purpose of Dogecoin In comparison, Dogecoin did not enter the market with those grand ideals in mind. Markus has stated that initially the coin was created as a joke. Like Bitcoin, his intentions are interwoven with the coin's characteristics. For example, the name Dogecoin and its now famous Shiba Inu logo were a reference to a meme popular at the time.

The coin did not originate with a divine purpose in mind, but rather to make people smile and make the select people who thought they would ever see the project laugh.

Despite its modest goals, Dogecoin has done a lot of good for people around the world. Not long after its launch, Dogecoin began to gain value. Since the project was originally started with a comical nature, the creators of the token felt it would be good humor to promote their good intentions by donating their profits to worthy causes around the world.

ONE COULD SAY that Dogecoin's goodwill began as soon as the coin hit the market. Almost miraculously, Dogecoin saw a 300% increase in value days after launch. The gains didn't hold for long, but they helped prove that there was a demand for a lighthearted and fun version of Bitcoin.

DESPITE ITS MODEST GOALS, Dogecoin has done a lot of good for people around the world. Not long after its launch, Dogecoin began to gain value. Since the project was originally started with a comical nature, the token's creators felt it would be good humor to promote their good intentions by donating their profits to worthy causes around the world.

ARGUABLY, Dogecoin's goodwill began as soon as the coin hit the market. Almost miraculously, Dogecoin saw a 300% increase in value days after launch. The gains didn't hold for long, but they helped prove that there was a demand for a lighthearted and fun version of Bitcoin.

DOGECOIN VS BITCOIN **- The first trick.**

DOGECOIN DIDN'T HAVE to be in service for long before its goodwill and community had a chance to further carve out its unique niche. In December 2013, just days after launch, the Dogecoin wallet was hacked. The insider stole millions of Dogecoin from a large user base. For most coins, such a devastating stunt would have signaled the end of the joke, however, for Dogecoin, it was its first true test.

AFTER THE HACK, Dogecoin organized a fundraising campaign under the name "SaveDOGEmas" in an effort to pay those who had incurred losses. Impressively, the community took up the challenge and, within days, all those who had lost coins saw their losses reimbursed through donations from other Dogecoin holders. This was the first, but not the last time, that Dogecoin's goodwill would help those less fortunate.

The successful payout of the stunt helped differentiate the coin from other first-generation projects at the time. It also encouraged the project's founders to see what other great causes they could champion. In 2014, the platform launched an impressive goodwill campaign that included raising $25,000.00 for the Jamaican Bobsled team. From there, the network became even more ambitious in its goals to make the world a better place.

## DOGECOIN BECOMES **a humanitarian**

THE FOLLOWING YEAR, the Dogecoin community stepped up its efforts significantly. That year, Dogecoin supporters helped sponsor a clean water initiative in Kenya with great success. From there, the community didn't stop. Their next campaign would help train assistance dogs for autistic children. Today, Dogecoin has an impressive track record of helping the less fortunate around the world. It is this spirit of goodwill that continually makes this coin a popular project.

. . .

## TECHNICAL DIFFERENCES

THERE IS no denying that Dogecoin shares many technical aspects with Bitcoin. However, they are not identical. There are some variations that make the two coins more than just duplicates. The founders of Dogecoin were able to weave their sense of humor into the coin's core coding. Specifically, they changed many of the terms used within the ecosystem. For example, Dogecoin miners are referred to as diggers.

## CONSENSUS

MARKUS ALSO CHANGED some aspects of the consensus mechanism when creating Dogecoin. Bitcoin relies on the SHA-256 consensus mechanism to protect its network. Dogecoin eliminates SHA-256 and instead relies on scrypt technology within its proof-of-work or Proof-Of-Work (PoW) mechanism. The change was a direct response to the increasingly competitive nature of the Bitcoin mining sector.

AT THE TIME, the Bitcoin mining sector was already experiencing heavy concentration. Miners had begun building more powerful GPU platforms and the entry of Bitmain's first ASIC (application-specific integrated chip) based miners in 2013 had sent the price of Bitcoin mining skyrocketing. These new miners were thousands of times more powerful than CPU-based miners.

Mining centralization Unfortunately, the new mining platforms were also expensive. This left Bitcoin mining only for those who had the funds to buy one of these high-powered machines. Of course, you could still mine the currency with your normal PC, as you still can today, however, the chances of receiving a reward in such a competitive mining sector were very low. In essence, these developments prevent the average user from participating in the protection of the Bitcoin blockchain.

EAGER TO AVOID a similar scenario with Dogecoin, Markus had the good foresight to use a scrypt-based Proof-Of-Work (PoW) algorithm. The advantage of this style of Proof-Of-Work (PoW) is that it prevents people from using their Bitcoin ASIC miners on the network. The strategy paid off because it leveled the playing field. You can only mine Dogecoin using FPGA devices and dedicated ASICs.

IN ADDITION, Dogecoin reduced block times compared to Bitcoin. Bitcoin miners approve blocks of new transactions in ten-minute intervals. Dogecoin diggers approve blocks every minute. This increased mining rate actually led to some problems later in Dogecoin's development. Originally, Dogecoin was intended to issue only 100 billion coins. However, block times of 10 minutes led to the network issuing all of its coins in 2015. The developers have now changed the protocol to issue 5 billion coins per year in the future.

Bitcoin is set at 21 million coins with the last Bitcoin rewards scheduled for issuance sometime in the year 2140. No more Bitcoin will ever be created beyond this point. It is this scarcity that adds to the overall value of the cryptocurrency. This is why a single Bitcoin can cost over $30,000.00 and a single Dogecoin costs around $0.30+ In terms of investment, both projects are exciting. Of course, there is no chance that Dogecoin will reach the astronomical values that Bitcoin may one day achieve. Mainly because there are many more Dogecoin on the market. However, that doesn't mean you can't get a serious ROI by investing in Dogecoin.

Dogecoin has a history of impressive market runs driven by its community and general goodwill. Recently, the coin skyrocketed in value 7x after receiving enthusiastic backing from some well-known celebrities and a popular Reddit investment group. This was not the first time Dogecoin had a breakout and probably won't be the last. In this way, Dogecoin represents the goodwill of the crypto community and the underlying goal of improving the lives of everyone in the world, not just the wealthy.

For these reasons, it is not a bad idea to have some of these two coins in your wallet. Bitcoin because it represents true financial freedom and a break from hundreds of years of financial manipulation at the hands of governments, and Dogecoin because it demonstrates a willingness to help those around you and bring a more joyful approach to finance.

Given the state of the market, it is safe to assume that cryptocurrencies like Bitcoin are on the verge of wide-scale adoption. This year, several major financial institutions have abandoned their fiat holdings and transferred their reserves to Bitcoin. Each time another company undergoes this conversion, the market soars to new heights. In turn, these companies reap huge profits.

FOR EXAMPLE, popular electric car company Tesla Motors recently invested $1.5 billion in Bitcoin. In 30 days, Tesla had made more profit from the increase in Bitcoin's value than selling its cars for the entire year. Since then, the company has stated that it intends to integrate Bitcoin further into its ecosystem by allowing users to pay for their car payments directly using the world's first cryptocurrency.

Dogecoin also appears to have a bright future ahead of it. The coin is quickly becoming one of the most well-known projects in the market. The coin was also backed by the world's richest man and Tesla Motors CEO Elon Musk. The coin has now taken a more revolutionary stance in the eyes of investors. Many people are investing in Dogecoin as a sign of their willingness to abandon the unfair stock trading practices exercised by the world's leading hedge funds.

Dogecoin continues to make headlines as more investors join the financial revolution. Recently, U.S. rapper and movie star Snoop Dogg tweeted about the coin. This skyrocketed Dogecoin's value by as much as 55%. He is not alone in the growing number of celebrities helping to build the community of this fun-filled project. Even rock star from the legendary band Kiss, Gene Simmons, recently tweeted a photo of the beloved Shiba Inu, declaring himself "The God Of DOGE." While it's common for Bitcoin experts to dismiss Dogecoin due to its comedic intentions, the project is still very much alive and has been doing its thing for nearly a decade. When you combine this fact with the overwhelming support the coin has, it's hard to imagine Dogecoin exiting the market. For these reasons, both Dogecoin and Bitcoin can be considered vital to the wider adoption of cryptocurrencies.

# THREE

# WHY DOGECOIN INVESTMENT IS SO PROFITABLE AND HOW TO TAKE ADVANTAGE OF IT

Let's recognize and understand that Dogecoin is a decentralized digital currency, which does not exist in a physical form and is not issued, operated or managed by any bank, financial entity or single organization. Dogecoin is a very accessible and not at all intimidating currency due to its own friendly nature, perhaps because of its very origin; which makes it close to everyone. Among other things, there are those who see Dogecoin as a virtual currency without very great expectations for the future; they consider it as it emerged: a joke. However, many people have been attracted by this cryptocurrency and have decided to invest in it, despite the fact that its creators have abandoned it.

. . .

FOR HAVING EMERGED as an improvised currency and as something not at all serious and for fun, many decide not to buy Dogecoin, while others do it to become part of the meme, which is not a Bitcoin-like asset and which is very cheap, taking day by day the unexpected seriousness. Obtaining Dogecoin is considered more as an expense than as an investment itself, a situation that makes it and has been placing it in a quite particular range of popularity.

INVESTING in Dogecoin for a significant number of buyers is perhaps a "to see" what can happen, what can change, how much can be earned; a "to see" how valuable it would be to buy DOGE; something like "to see" if my lottery number comes out. Now, if nothing happens with the investment, then this would become just a purchase for fun, in making a recreational acquisition for pleasure or mere enjoyment.

Simply put, nothing happens. Its current price attracts and continues to capture the attention of the crypto investing public. For the time being, if someone considers investing in DOGE; it is advisable to see it as an expense and not exactly as an investment itself, perhaps when you least expect it; the moment of its glory arrives. You may hear all kinds of stories in the investment process that increase your Fear Of Missing Out (FOMO), your fear of missing an opportunity, that emotional feeling of dread that affects all investors.

You will hear stories of successes and failures, of triumphs and defeats, maybe there are more negative stories than positive ones and this generates a lot of fear and insecurity. Remember, opportunity comes and knocks at your door, open and let it pass; make up your mind to take that big step.

With the passing of days and this short period of time that Dogecoin has been on the cryptocurrency path, it has managed to position itself very well and create attraction in the market. Remember that it is feasible to invest in this virtual currency, that yes; considered a possible risk, but at the same time a great opportunity; that is to say, your investment can bear fruit as well as it could be sterile. In the meantime, DOGE continues to grow, gaining value and market capitalization. This is not bingo, but we are venturing into a world where anything could happen.

DOGECOIN HAS BEEN and remains in the headlines for the past few months for its staggering returns. Since the beginning of the year, Dogecoin's price has skyrocketed by nearly 7,000% at the time of this writing. In the past 12 months, it has increased by more than 15,500%.

COMPARED to two of the biggest and most popular names in crypto, Bitcoin (CRYPTO: BTC) and Ethereum (CRYPTO: ETH), have seen their prices increase by around 300% and 1,000%, respectively, over the past year 2020. While many cryptocurrencies have experienced record returns, Dogecoin is in a growth and development league all its own.

IT'S hard to ignore numbers like these. However, just because an investment is earning such high returns doesn't necessarily mean it's a good idea to buy. Dogecoin may be too good to be true, and there is a lot of risk to consider before investing.

A low price is not always good or timely, even more so in the realm of cryptocurrencies like Bitcoin and Ethereum, which may be the biggest players in the crypto space, but are also expensive. In mid-April of this year, when Bitcoin peaked, it cost around $65,000 per token. Ethereum cost just over $4,000 per token at its peak in mid-May of the same year.

. . .

HOWEVER, Dogecoin's record high was just $0.68. With such a low price, it's one of the most affordable investments out there. And if you're unsure about investing, it can be tempting to buy Dogecoin simply because it's cheap, nothing more.

ON THE OTHER HAND, that can be an incredibly risky move because affordable investments aren't always the best ones to make. If you buy Dogecoin just because it's cheaper than its competitors, you could still end up losing money, and of this there is no doubt in the world.

WHILE ALL CRYPTOCURRENCIES ARE RISKY, Dogecoin is one of the most dangerous investments. Before even considering buying, it is important to think about how this investment can prove to be effective and the most convenient over time.

MANY OF US would like to have a big crystal ball and rather than predict the future, know their Dogecoin will survive in the long run. With any investment, the most important factor to consider is whether it is likely to experience long-term growth. Long-term investments are more likely to recover after recessions and retain a competitive advantage in their industry.

CRYPTOCURRENCIES, in general, remain highly speculative. In other words, no one knows for sure whether they will still be around in a few years or decades. Dogecoin, however, is especially risky because it does not have as much utility as its competitors.

·  ·  ·

FOR ANY CRYPTOCURRENCY TO become commonplace, it must have some kind of real-world use. Bitcoin is the most popular type of cryptocurrency, and it is the type of cryptocurrency that traders are most willing to accept. That gives it a significant advantage because widespread adoption will be key to the success of any cryptocurrency.

ETHEREUM ALSO HAS REAL-WORLD utility through its Blockchain technology.

The Ethereum blockchain not only hosts its native token, Ether, but is also the network used by non-fungible tokens (NFT), decentralized finance and thousands of other applications. Ethereum technology has the potential to revolutionize a variety of industries and, if successful, its cryptocurrency, Ether, also has a good chance of thriving.

Dogecoin, on the other hand, has very little utility at the moment. The few merchants that accept crypto are more likely to accept Bitcoin than Dogecoin, and Dogecoin has no significant advantages over its competitors at present.

ANOTHER BIG QUESTION IS, whether the price of Dogecoin will continue to rise. Of course, despite having very little real-world utility, Dogecoin's returns have still outperformed its competitors. However, those gains are largely artificial and probably won't last forever.

Part of the reason Dogecoin's price has skyrocketed is because it has been heavily promoted and produced online. Famous billionaires like Elon Musk and Mark Cuban have spread Dogecoin on social media, and retail investors have invested in droves.

·  ·  ·

THE MORE PEOPLE invest in an asset, the higher its price. The Dogecoin run is similar to the GameStop saga earlier this year when investors bid up the stock price only to dump it shortly thereafter in an attempt to make a quick buck.

WITH ANY INVESTMENT, if the stock price doesn't align with the underlying fundamentals, that's a red flag. Dogecoin has little utility and no competitive advantage in the industry, yet its price has skyrocketed. That is a likely sign that this growth may not continue over the long term, something that remains to be seen.

DOGECOIN'S PRICE has already worsened in recent weeks. And unless it develops a way to stay competitive, it is very likely, according to some experts, that it will not survive over time. So, no matter how inexpensive it is, it's still a dangerous investment.

Now, if you don't invest in Dogecoin, where should you. Whether you choose to invest in cryptocurrencies or stocks, it's always a good idea to research the underlying fundamentals of an investment. Look beyond the price and try to determine if the investment has real-world utility and a strong competitive advantage.

THE BEST INVESTMENTS are the ones that are most likely to experience long-term growth. Dogecoin may not be the best investment right now, but there are many safer options that still have the potential for higher returns.

IT IS a matter of very personal interest to know if now is the time to invest or risk $1,000 in Dogecoin, bearing in mind the backing of large and loyal investor-fans including major celebrities and brands. It would be timely, before investing in Dogecoin, it would not hurt to appreciate the fact that a large group of industry experts and analysts have compiled a list of what they consider to be the 10 best stocks for investors to buy at this time, and curiously, Dogecoin is not one of them.

THE WEB INVESTMENT service that has managed for almost two decades Motley Fool Stock Advisor, has beaten the stock market for more than 4 times, and right now, they believe that there are 10 stocks that represent the best investment option and, why not; using your digital funds. Let's take a look at this interesting list, which does not include any cryptocurrency, but constitutes a group of those that you can make use of:

## MERCADOLIBRE, **Inc.**

OPERATES ONLINE TRADING platforms in Latin America. Mercado Pago FinTech, Mercado Fondo and Mercado Crédito are all important pillars. The company also offers Mercado Shops, an online storefront solution, which allows users to set up, manage and promote their own web stores. The company was incorporated in 1999 and is headquartered in Buenos Aires, Argentina.

## SEA LIMITED

Together with its subsidiaries, it is engaged in the digital entertainment, e-commerce and digital financial services businesses in Southeast Asia, Latin America, the rest of Asia and internationally. Sea Limited was incorporated in 2009 and is headquartered in Singapore.

· · ·

## COUPANG, **Inc.**

OWNS and operates e-commerce businesses through its mobile applications and Internet websites primarily in South Korea. The company was founded in 2010 and is headquartered in Seoul, South Korea.

## JUMIA TECHNOLOGIES AG

Operates an e-commerce platform in Africa. The company was formerly known as Africa Internet Holding GmbH and changed its name to Jumia Technologies AG in January 2019. Jumia Technologies AG was founded in 2012 and is headquartered in Berlin, Germany.

## SHOPIFY INC.

A COMMERCE COMPANY, provides a commerce platform and services. The company's platform offers merchants the ability to manage their businesses across multiple sales channels. The company was formerly known as Jaded Pixel Technologies Inc. and changed its name to Shopify Inc. in November 2011. Shopify Inc. was incorporated in 2004 and is headquartered in Ottawa, Canada.

## ALIBABA GROUP HOLDING LIMITED.

THROUGH ITS SUBSIDIARIES, it offers mobile and online commerce businesses in the People's Republic of China and internationally. It operates through four segments: Core Commerce, Cloud

Computing, Digital Media and Entertainment, and Innovation Initiatives and Others. The company was founded in 1999 and is headquartered in Hangzhou, People's Republic of China.

## VIPSHOP HOLDINGS LIMITED

IT OPERATES as an online discount retailer for various brands in the People's Republic of China. It operates through four segments, Vip.com, Shan Outlets, Internet Finance and others. The company was founded in 2008 and is headquartered in Guangzhou, People's Republic of China.

## GLOBAL-E ONLINE LTD.

OPERATES an e-commerce platform that connects online retailers and brands with customers around the world. The company was incorporated in 2013 and is headquartered in Israel and London, United Kingdom. It has additional offices in New York, New York; Paris, France; Petah Tikva, Israel; Beverly Hills, California; Atlanta, Georgia.

## BETTERWARE DE MÉXICO, **S.A.B. de C.V.**

OPERATES as a direct consumer company in Mexico. The company focuses on the home organization segment. It serves approximately 3 million households through distributors and associates in approximately 800 communities throughout Mexico. Betterware was founded in 1995 and is headquartered in Zapopan, Mexico. Betterware de México, S.A.B. de C.V. is a subsidiary of Campalier, S.A. de C.V.

## OZON HOLDINGS PLC

Together with its subsidiaries, operates as an Internet retailer of multi-category consumer products to the general public, primarily in the Russian Federation. The company offers products in various categories including electronics, home and décor products, children's items, fast-moving consumer goods, fresh food, and automotive parts. It also operates an online marketplace platform that enables third-party sellers. Ozon Holdings PLC was incorporated in 1999 and is based in Nicosia, Cyprus.

A BASIC RANGE of companies and great opportunities globally, where your cryptocurrency investment will undoubtedly benefit. This is not a list of other crypto, but of companies that, through the digital world, have firmly established themselves, making it possible for the use and investment of your electronic money to be seen and perceived as profitable, in favor of your cryptographic activity.

CRYPTOCURRENCIES ARE MOVING THE PLANET; and how!

## BUYING **Dogecoin**

THE FIRST STEP to buying Dogecoin is to open an account with a cryptocurrency exchange that supports DOGE. Dogecoin is available on Coinbase, eToro, Robinhood, Gemini and Webull.

After both your wallet and exchange account are open, you can place a purchase order to buy DOGE. First, open your exchange's trading platform and look at the current price of DOGE. Although cryptocurrency prices are always changing, you can expect to pay close to the market rate; you may want to keep track of the price of DOGE and how it is moving to make sure you don't overpay for your coins.

The best exchanges will offer you a wide range of order types to choose from. If you've ever traded stocks before, you're probably already familiar with the basic types of orders. If you haven't, be sure to familiarize yourself with the most common order types before investing. Choose an order type and calculate the amount of DOGE you want to buy based on your available funds and the current market price.

FROM HERE, your broker will complete the order on your behalf. When you see your DOGE in your exchange wallet, it means your order has been completed. If your broker is unable to complete your order according to your specifications, you can cancel it at the end of the trading day.

A cryptocurrency wallet provides you with a set of keys that you can use to store your DOGE outside of an exchange. This helps keep your investment safer in case your exchange is hacked or stolen.

Robinhood currently does not offer users access to send or receive their assets to another wallet. If you want to own your own cryptocurrency, use a wallet that allows you to control your own private key. Coinbase, eToro and Gemini provide access to send and receive from their respective exchange wallets. For added security, use a wallet that allows you to manage your own private key.

THERE ARE 2 main types of cryptocurrency wallets:
hot software wallets and cold hardware storage wallets. Software wallets are free, but must be connected to the Internet to access your

investments. Hardware wallets store your coins offline for maximum security, but can cost up to $50. Consider your favorite software and hardware wallet options when deciding how you'll store your DOGE.

HERE ARE the best crypto exchanges for Dogecoin.

- GEMINI: New investors.

- ETORO: Cryptocurrency trading.

- ROBINHOOD: Buying and selling Dogecoin.

- WEBULL: Intermediate traders and investors.

- VOYAGER: Mobile traders.

- COINBASE: Earn rewards.

IT IS essential that you have the right application for this purpose, where you can buy your Dogecoins with security, confidence and peace of mind. One of the main exchanges that can provide you with this wonderful opportunity, for you to make inroads into the DOGE community, is Binance.

Now, what is Binance?

.  .  .

BINANCE IS one of the most recognized and popular exchange plat-forms in the world for the large number of digital currencies offered on the network, and its very low and characteristic commissions for transactions made, which provides a service for buying and selling different cryptocurrencies, based on the daily values determined by the crypto market.

THE BRILLIANT MIND behind this exchange is Changpeng Zhao, a Chinese-Canadian entrepreneur and founder of the company, which is currently the largest virtual currency exchange platform on the planet, backed by the large volume of transactions carried out per day.

Binance was created in China for the month of July 2017 with funding of $15 million, which were raised during an initial coin offering (ICO). A few months after its founding, Binance was forced to move its offices to Japan because the local government banned all cryptocurrency trading. By March 2018, Binance was already posi-tioned as the exchange with the largest number of transactions and operations worldwide, with offices in Japan and Taiwan. In addition to important project alliances in Bermuda, Malta, Israel and part of Europe.

THIS EXCHANGE HAS the joy of boasting that for the year 2018 it had the largest and biggest crypto exchange in history with a market capitalization of BNB of 1.3 billion dollars. Reason why Zhao, the current CEO of Binance, had the opportunity to be rated by the specialists of Forbes magazine as the third richest person in the world in cryptocurrencies.

Changpeng Zhao sees clearly and is very aware of the future of the crypto world. That is why his determination is forceful. "Binance is ready to survive any number of years, regardless of whether it is bear or bull (...) Our target is much longer than another year. Our goal is 10, 50, 100 years. So we will be here for a while," he once said.

BINANCE ALLOWS its users to trade and trade (investment in the market with the aim of making a profit) in real time with more than 100 cryptocurrencies.

AT OUR POINT, we are interested in how to buy Dogecoin. Well, the first step you need to take, is to register and create a personal account on Binance, which can be done from a computer or a mobile device, which is completely free and is available worldwide. For registration, you only need an email address and a password.

ONCE WE ARE on the main page, Binance will show us on the upper right side the options "Login" and "Register". This button (Registration), will take us to one that we will have to fill out with the data requested there.

UPON COMPLETING OUR REGISTRATION, Binance will proceed to send an email confirming the request to create a new account. The link that arrives in this message will give the approval and verification of the new user registration and with it the possibility to start using the Binance exchange with total freedom.

IT SHOULD BE NOTED that Binance can be used from any type of device or operating system, and is available in 15 languages, including Spanish, English, French, German, Portuguese and Italian.

Once inside our own Binance user account, we are invited to select a series of recommendations that the same platform offers us to continue safely and then give an answer if we consider activating the two-factor authentication:

Google Authenticator or SMS (text message). It is important to know that this last step is not mandatory; it is at the user's discretion. However, it is recommended to do so, since it provides more and better security for safe and optimal use of the Binance platform.

Knowing Binance, knowing that it is the most popular and recognized exchange in the world for the immense number of cryptocurrencies it operates and the amount of transactions made daily; you have at hand the most suitable resource to buy, among other currencies; your Dogecoins with total safety, security and guarantee. A platform with the lowest commissions, operative in practically all devices and versions, multilingual and with the widest geographical spectrum.

Here your investments for fun, curiosity or seriousness are very well supported, since they enjoy the prestige and support of a platform with total credibility and seriousness in the network and the cryptoverse. So do not stop and leave aside the possibility of entering into doubts, trust your instincts, rely on great resources and avoid FOMO.

## WHICH WALLETS SUPPORT THIS CRYPTOCURRENCY?

STORING cryptocurrencies on an exchange is not recommended, as it increases the risk of being hacked. Since centralized exchanges maintain custody of your funds, they are great targets for cryptocurrency hackers. If a hacker can breach the exchange, they could steal the funds held on the platform. To mitigate this risk, you should use a cryptocurrency wallet that allows you to maintain custody of your cryptocurrency.

.  .  .

## Ellipal Titan

IT IS a multi-currency wallet that supports DOGE, Bitcoin, Ethereum and more than 7,000 additional digital assets. The Ellipal Titan features a large touchscreen that makes it easy to keep track of your holdings without connecting to Wi-Fi. Since the wallet is not connected to the Internet, it is impossible for online hackers to steal your assets. To transfer your coins to your wallet, you can use the device's QR to send cryptocurrencies in a matter of seconds. With a simple, streamlined interface and a straightforward setup process, Ellipal Titan is an ideal choice for cryptocurrency investors.

ELLIPAL TITAN generally commands a premium over other cryptocurrency wallets, as it has several premium features that enhance the user experience.

## Dogecoin Wallet

THE FUN and friendly Internet currency also offers its own simple and intuitive wallet option for both desktop computers and mobile devices. Getting started with Dogecoin Wallet takes approximately 5 minutes. Simply click on your operating system, download and run the wallet and start storing your DOGE securely online. You can also download Dogecoin Wallet for free from the Google Play store.

AFTER SEEING your DOGE in your exchange wallet, you will now need to decide how you want to get a return on your investment. There are 2 main strategies you can take:

·  ·  ·

## LONG-TERM HOLDING:

INVESTORS WHO BELIEVE that the price of Dogecoin can hold it for months or even years at a time. If this is your strategy, transfer your DOGE to your wallet as soon as possible to keep your investments safer.

Short-term scalping: short-term investors capitalize on small price movements by buying and selling DOGE when it is advantageous for them.

IF YOU PLAN to become a short-term investor, it is important to have access to a reliable and fast-executing trading platform.

IT IS important to be aware of the price of cryptocurrencies, as it can vary second by second. Some of the factors that can influence the price you will pay to invest in DOGE or another cryptocurrency may include:

- CURRENT SUPPLY: There is a rapidly dwindling supply of DOGE available, although 10,000 DOGE are minted with each block, about 1 minute.

- NEWS: Elon Musk hosted the SNL TV Show for the first time and much of the anticipation will focus on his decision to include Dogecoin in a skit.

·  ·  ·

- CURRENT FINANCIAL CONDITIONS: Investors tend to flock to alternative investments such as cryptocurrency when the overall market is trending downward.

POOR ECONOMIC CONDITIONS can drive up the price of DOGE.

Monitoring how the prices of other cryptocurrencies are moving can help you decide when you should place your buy order. Explore cryptocurrency market conditions using our live benchmark chart.

WHETHER YOU DECIDE to invest in Dogecoin, Bitcoin or another major cryptocurrency, remember the risks involved in buying a volatile asset. The cryptocurrency market is still largely unregulated and the price of any cryptocurrency can drop in value at any time. Never invest more money than you can afford to lose and use cryptocurrency as a complement to a diversified portfolio.

Before you can begin to experience and venture into the world of cryptocurrencies, it is necessary to open a Dogecoin wallet. By using your own wallet, you will be able to store and send Dogecoin to any user anywhere in the world. It is important to understand the purpose of owning a Dogecoin wallet and the purpose it serves. There are different types of Dogecoin wallets, fully recommended so you can buy and/or sell your DOGEs freely.

A Dogecoin wallet can be both physical and digital, it keeps your public and private keys and connects to the ledger or Blockchain. Your wallet's public key, which also serves as your wallet address, is like your Dogecoin bank account number, where anyone can track transactions made, but no one will be able to know who they belong to or that they are yours. You can access your public key balance through your wallet's private key, which is used to approve transactions on the Blockchain.

. . .

THERE IS a diversity of Dogecoin wallets available, from which you can choose the one of your preference. The options differ from online wallets accessible through the web to hardware wallets that are a bit more expensive.

THERE ARE JUST over 70 wallets that support Dogecoin, which can give you an idea of how this joke has been taken very seriously on the web. Through the web you have the opportunity to visualize, compare and qualify the wallets of your preference and go discarding until you select the one of your preference and that covers all your expectations and needs. You will have the facility to make a comparison between types of wallets, supported cryptocurrencies and price, using a table of similarities and differences.

## WHAT TO LOOK **for in a Dogecoin wallet?**

WHEN LOOKING for the best Dogecoin wallet that truly meets your needs, remember to look out for the following features:

## DOGE SUPPORT.

BEFORE ANALYZING the features of a wallet, check well what we call "the fine print" and thus be able to make sure that the wallet you choose is truly DOGE compatible.

## EASE OF USE
If you're new to digital currencies or simply don't handle the technology with great skill, look for a user-friendly wallet designed for

those new to cryptocurrencies. A simple user interface can make managing your coins much easier and less stressful.

## SECURITY

WHAT SECURITY FEATURES does the wallet offer? For example, does it offer hot or cold storage? Does it include 2-factor authentication and/or multi-sig functionality? Have you ever had any reported media security breaches?

## BACKUP AND RESTORE

IS it easy to back up the wallet and then restore it if necessary, making sure you don't lose any coins if something goes wrong?

Ongoing development Research the development team behind the wallet to find out if they are constantly working on updates and improvements to the wallet's features and functionality.

## CUSTOMER SUPPORT

IF YOU EVER ENCOUNTER A PROBLEM WITH your wallet or a particular transaction, how can you contact customer service? Check the contact options available and investigate whether the wallet provider has a good reputation for responding quickly to calls for help.

## POSITIVE REVIEWS

Don't simply rely on a wallet provider's marketing comments; Check out independent online reviews from other users to find out their opinions on the pros and cons of a wallet, and would they recommend it from new users.

THE WORLD of cryptocurrencies is really interesting. Since the inception of Bitcoin, several peculiar projects have appeared here and there. One of the most unique projects is Dogecoin: if you're a DOGE enthusiast, you'll be happy to know that, in this list, we'll be looking for the best Dogecoin wallet of the year.

BEING as unique as it is, I would expect Dogecoin to have some. Well, less than common storage options. However, the truth is quite the opposite - DOGE is a beloved cryptocurrency, and as such, some of the best crypto wallets on the market offer support for this digital currency.

BEFORE WE GET into the contrarieties of the best Dogecoin wallets, it's a good idea to have a quick review of what DOGE really is and what attracts people to the project.

NOW, truth be told, Dogecoin is unique, without using the word lightly. While most other cryptocurrency projects have some specific high-level goals they aim to achieve or some specific problems they aim to solve, DOGE is different. Very different, in fact.

DOGECOIN WAS CREATED as a joke cryptocurrency. Hence its name, hence the reputation behind it. There are no noble causes that the community behind DOGE is interested in; for lack of a better term, it is a "troll cryptocurrency."

HOWEVER, that being the case, why are so many people looking for Dogecoin wallets and ways to buy DOGE?

WHILE THE CRYPTOCURRENCY IS A JOKE, literally speaking, there is a rather interesting dichotomy here. The Dogecoin community is one of the most active and communicative crypto groups you will ever come across. This makes it a very unique community.

ON TOP OF THAT, being active isn't just a gimmick either. DOGE enthusiasts participate in fundraising events, community projects and various charity events. It's a very unique phenomenon in the crypto world.

However, be aware that since DOGE is such a peculiar crypto project, it comes with some caveats. The coin is loved by pump-and-dumpers: people who love to manipulate the market, artificially inflate the price of a specific cryptocurrency and then dump all their coins, causing its price to collapse exponentially.

Make sure you don't fall prey to such dishonest players. Your best option is to set a specific goal of why you want to invest in Dogecoin and then use the services of the best Dogecoin wallets out there. Don't allow third parties to influence your opinions - do your research and be diligent.

SO, we've established what Dogecoin is and what the cryptocurrency behind it is primarily used for. Naturally, however, anyone who wants to buy some DOGE will need a reliable wallet to hold their coins. That's exactly what we're about to review:

Let's start by taking a look at the different types of Dogecoin wallets that are available.

## TYPES OF DOGECOIN wallets

LIKE MANY OTHER cryptocurrencies on the market, Dogecoin can be stored in a wide selection of different wallets; we've already established that. However, as you can probably guess, not all wallets are created equal: some will be better than others, either from a security standpoint or simply because of the user's personal preferences.

IN GENERAL, you should know that there are two major types of wallets available to access and use: cold and hot wallets. Let's explore what these terms mean, specifically, so that when we get to listing the best real Dogecoin wallets, you know what we're talking about.

## CONVENIENT AND ACCESSIBLE HOT WALLETS.

A "HOT WALLET" is a type of cryptocurrency wallet that maintains a constant connection to the Internet. The definition itself is quite broad, as is the category: a hot wallet could be a mobile app, a browser extension, downloadable software, or anything in between.

THE VAST MAJORITY of crypto enthusiasts you're likely to communicate with will probably tell you that they're using a hot wallet for their cryptocurrency storage needs, including DOGE. That's because of the wide range of these wallets available; as you'll see in just a minute, cold storage has a much less varied selection of options.

## NOW, **what makes hot wallets so popular?**

WELL, no matter if you're looking for the best wallet for Dogecoin or any other cryptocurrency, probably the first thing you'll notice is the accessibility and convenience factors of these wallets. Frankly, hot wallets are available to everyone.

WHAT WE MEAN to tell you by that is that hot wallets are usually completely free to use and can be set up in a matter of minutes. Whether it's an exchange-based wallet or a software wallet, they are usually accompanied by clear and concise instructions, and are super simple to get started with.

As for convenience, if you choose a hot wallet as your choices for the best Dogecoin wallet of the year, you can rest assured that you'll be able to access their funds, check their balances, and make 'send' and 'receive' orders at the touch of a button. This is especially true with Dogecoin mobile wallets, as we have our phones with us wherever we go, so you'll always have your DOGE at hand.

However, hot wallets come with a trade-off. In short, they will never be as secure as cold storage of cryptocurrencies; that's just the way it is. It all comes down to the whole "connecting to the Internet" thing: with a constant web connection, hackers have plenty of opportunities to breach the security of an active wallet and steal your funds in the process.

Naturally, this is not as common an occurrence today, but it still happens. That said, however, this is exactly where cold wallets come in.

. . .

## COLD WALLETS SECURITY AND RELIABILITY.

COLD WALLETS ARE those cryptographic storage options that don't have a constant connection to the Internet; after the definition of hot wallet, you've probably seen this one coming.

HOWEVER, it's true: the only time you would connect your cold wallet to the web is when you want to transfer your funds or buy more cryptocurrencies.

NOW, when looking for the best Dogecoin wallet, you can definitely expect cold wallets to pop up quite often. That's also the case with most other cryptocurrencies: no matter what the coin is, if a cold wallet supports it, it will be recommended to you.

COLD WALLETS OFFER users unparalleled security features. Whether it is a hardware device, a paper wallet or anything else, cold wallets will surely give you the "best return for your investment".

ONE OF THE main things that deter people from using cold wallets is the price tag on these devices. It's not something you should worry about when it comes to paper wallets, but at the same time, these are the most specific cold storage options, so they are not too relevant to specify in this interesting article.

. . .

ASIDE FROM THE PRICE TAG, the only other reason some people might prefer an online Dogecoin wallet over a cold one is due to the steep learning curve that comes with some hardware devices. If DOGE is the first cryptocurrency you own, it can be difficult to figure out some of the intricacies of certain hardware wallets. Definitely not all of them.

THAT SAID, at this point, we should now be somewhat clearer and more understood about cold and hot wallets, Cold-Hot Wallets and the main differences between them. Which we will now expose to you as the main ones that support our fun coin Dogecoin.

## MEET **the top ten (10) wallets to hold Dogecoin**

## LEDGER NANO X

THE LEDGER NANO X is one of the most popular cold wallets on the market. In fact, one could go so far as to argue that it is the most popular cold wallet; this is true for both Dogecoin and other cryptocurrencies. There are quite a few aspects that also attribute to this.

FOR STARTERS, if you are looking for the best Dogecoin wallet, you are probably concerned about the security of your DOGE coins, if that is the case, then Ledgar Nano X is a perfect choice, as it offers unprecedented levels of security.

WHILE SETTING up your Nano X, you will be prompted to create a PIN code that you will need to enter every time you want to access your digital assets. This is accompanied by a 24-word recovery seed: if you forget your PIN at any point, you can still retrieve your Dogecoins with this seed.

## Trezor Model T

THIS IS one of the leading cold wallet brands in the cryptocurrency world. The company's products can be consistently found on lists of the best cryptocurrency wallets; naturally, they can also be considered among the best Dogecoin wallets.

THIS IS ESPECIALLY true with the Trezor Model T, Trezor's latest and greatest. The wallet features a few distinct aspects that any DOGE lover will surely appreciate.

FOR STARTERS, the Trezor Model T is undoubtedly one of the most secure cryptocurrency wallets you can buy with money. It is equipped with all the top-notch security features and uses some virtually unbreakable defenses. Backup features, firmware update requests, PIN codes, you name it.

## Trezor One

Trezor One is the previous version of one of the leading hardware wallets in the crypto industry: the Trezor Model T. As you've probably noticed, both models have also made their way into our list of the best Dogecoin wallets.

Now, just because Trezor One is the older wallet and there is a new and improved version available doesn't mean it's obsolete. On the contrary, the Trezor One model still has a very specific group of cryptocurrency enthusiasts that it caters to in spades.

FOR STARTERS, in true Trezor fashion, you can expect this best wallet option for Dogecoin to be very secure. It has advanced PIN code functionality that, in addition to a limited USB connection, prevents your DOGE coins from being stolen by a keylogger or some other malware that may be present on your computer.

## BINANCE

IF YOU ARE familiar with the world of cryptocurrencies, you have probably heard of Binance. It's one of the most popular cryptocurrency exchange platforms out there worldwide.

YES, you read that right: a crypto exchange. However, it's an exchange that can also act as an online Dogecoin wallet. And a pretty good one, to boot.

BINANCE IS DEFINITELY A HOT WALLET, as far as DOGE storage is concerned. You would keep your coins in your Binance account, which simply acts as a wallet.

Many users and also DOGE users will tell you that Dogecoin storage like this should be temporary, that you should always opt to buy a hardware cryptocurrency wallet and transfer your funds to it as soon as possible. Well, that's completely correct; however, storing your DOGE on Binance has some notable benefits.

. . .

THESE BENEFITS WILL BE IMMEDIATELY clear to those DOGE holders who plan to actively trade their coins, hoping to profit while doing so. If you are a trader yourself (or striving to become one), Binance could be the best Dogecoin wallet for you.

## LEDGER NANO S (HARDWARE WALLET).

Multiple cryptocurrency storage, good security features, simple and easy to use For secure cryptocurrency storage, most users recommend offline storage. One offline storage option worth considering is Ledger Nano S, a popular hardware wallet that boasts a number of security features.

THIS SMALL USB device stores your private keys in a PIN-protected secure item, and also has an easy backup and restore feature along with support for 2-factor authentication. There is a built-in OLED display that, along with the device's buttons that must be physically pressed, can be used to verify transactions manually.

THE SETUP PROCESS for the Nano S is quick and easy, and the device supports more than 20 cryptocurrencies, including among them Dogecoin, Bitcoin, Ethereum, Dash and Litecoin.

THE MAIN DRAWBACK of this handy little device is the cost. Like any hardware wallet, it comes at a price.

KeepKey (Hardware Wallet) Security, can store multiple cryptocurrencies. KeepKey is another leading player in the hardware wallet sector. Launched in 2015, this cold storage wallet supports multiple cryptocurrencies as well as Dogecoin, including Bitcoin, Ethereum and Dash, and places a strong emphasis on security.

. . .

BEING A HIERARCHICAL DETERMINISTIC (HD) WALLET, KeepKey allows you to generate and store an unlimited number of private keys. The device is PIN-protected and has a large display to track transactions.

ALL TRANSACTIONS MUST BE CONFIRMED MANUALLY with a button on the device. You can exchange assets directly on your KeepKey using ShapeShift, and your wallet works on PC, Mac, Linux and Android operating systems.

HOWEVER, you'll have to shell out more for KeepKey than for other wallets, which means it may not be an ideal option for some DOGE holders.

Jaxx (Mobile and desktop wallet) Multi-coin and token storage, accessible on a wide range of devices, simple user interface. A multi-coin wallet that can be accessed on multiple devices, Jaxx is another popular choice for anyone looking to store Dogecoin.

Launched in 2014 and later rebranded as Jaxx Liberty, this wallet supports Dogecoin, Bitcoin, Ethereum, Litecoin, Dash, Zcash and dozens of other coins and tokens, so it's worth considering if you're looking to store a wide range of cryptocurrencies.

It's also worth a look if you want the convenience of cross-platform access. You can use Jaxx on your desktop (Windows, Mac and Linux operating systems), mobile devices (Android and iOS devices) and via a Chrome browser extension.

JAXX ALLOWS you to keep control of your private keys, and new users will have no problem managing their coins and tokens through Jaxx. The built-in ShapeShift functionality is another convenient feature.

The main disadvantage of Jaxx is that it is not immune to security issues. The June 2017 news of a $400,000 cryptocurrency theft due to a Jaxx wallet "vulnerability" reinforces the importance of maximizing security when managing your cryptocurrency coins.

## Kraken

KRAKEN IS PRIMARILY a cryptocurrency exchange platform. What this means is that you can exchange and trade various cryptos on the site; DOGE is no exception. However, Kraken can act perfectly well as an online Dogecoin wallet in addition to being an exchange.

THE WAY this works is quite simple. You have two great options: one where you already own some Dogecoins and one where you don't have any DOGE yet, but have decided you want to invest in it.

IF YOU ALREADY HAVE SOME Dogecoins at your disposal, depending on where they are, you can easily transfer them to your Kraken account, assuming you have created one. Just like any other high-end cryptocurrency exchange, it will simply navigate to the wallet (storage) part of your account and generate a DOGE wallet from there.

HOWEVER, if you don't own any Dogecoins yet and are looking for the best Dogecoin wallet to start your crypto journey on the right foot, the process will be even simpler. Frankly, all you need to do is sign up with Kraken and then buy some Dogecoins; they will be automatically credited to your Kraken account, and you can go from there.

Now, we have established that Kraken is easy to use and that you can store your Dogecoins on the platform. However, we still need to discuss the question of why you would want to do so in the first place.

KRAKEN IS all about a single feature: security. It can easily be named as one of the most secure cryptocurrency exchange sites on the market. Whether it's SSL certificates and login confirmations, or 2FA and cold storage services, you can be sure that Kraken will protect your cryptocurrencies pretty firmly.

That last part is also crucial. Kraken stores up to 95% of its users' funds on cold storage devices; think Ledger or Trezor, but at a major corporate level. This is absolutely fantastic, as it means no hacker will be able to access your Dogecoins.

If you are interested in what Kraken has to offer, it has caught your attention and you think this particular cryptocurrency exchange platform could be the best Dogecoin wallet for you, be sure to check it out in more detail.

## COINOMI (MOBILE WALLET)

MULTIPLE CRYPTOCURRENCY STORAGE, easy to use, HD wallet, built-in ShapeShift exchange. The features may be overkill if you just want a basic wallet.

Coinomi is an easy-to-use mobile wallet that provides a number of useful features for DOGE buyers. With a focus on quick and easy cryptocurrency management, this popular app supports more than 1,000 cryptocurrencies, including Dogecoin, Bitcoin, Ethereum, Dash and Zcash.

Coinomi, an HD wallet, is quick to set up and allows you to store your private keys on your device. You can start sending and receiving payments in just a few simple steps, and there's a built-in ShapeShift exchange for additional functionality.

You also don't have to go through any Know Your Customer (KYC) red tape to manage your funds, which is an important feature for anyone who values their anonymity.

Dogecoin Wallet (Desktop and Mobile) An "official" DOGE wallet. While you can still find and download the "official" Dogecoin wallet, it's not the smartest option. It is no longer actively supported or worked with, and many people have reported losing funds after using this wallet.

AS YOU CAN SEE, we only mention and offer a brief detail of 5 of the many existing wallets and of the 70 that support Dogecoin. It is up to the user to choose and keep the one that meets his expectations and, fundamentally, his operational needs, providing security and protection to his funds.

Even if they are invested for fun, they deserve protection, care and attention; a way to gain prestige and trust, reflecting in the market the relevance that a wallet can acquire, through the performance of work, advice and optimal and adequate attention; adjusted to each interest, although global; particular.

BENEFITS AND IMPORTANCE of owning a wallet for Dogecoin and your other cryptocurrencies

A CRYPTOCURRENCY WALLET allows users to send and receive cryptocurrencies and have a balance of cryptocurrencies. This type of wallet is necessary to make transactions of these coins online, as they can take place on Blockchain technology, which improves security. Managing multiple cryptocurrencies is also a possibility with a large number of wallets available.

. . .

CUSTOM WALLETS PROVIDE MORE scope control and flexibility to manage cryptocurrencies. It is suggested that you choose a custom application, provided by a reliable partner such as Inn4-science, as it has a better cryptocurrency wallet development that allows you to customize its features.

## A LONG-TERM SOLUTION

TECHNOLOGY DOES NOT DEVELOP OVERNIGHT. It takes innovations in innovations to grow through various stages of development. Cryptocurrencies are not available for everyone to use as of now, but it has extended its reach in most parts and is expected to grow widely in the coming years. Different transmission methods are being experimented with.

WITH THE TRUST of several large companies and acceptance as a payment method, cryptocurrency wallets are becoming more and more reliable. Cryptocurrency wallets can be a long-term solution for both investment and spending, allowing global transactions to be made more easily over the long term.

No conversion issues While the exchange could be made in different currencies, you are only entitled to use the converted value of that currency in your country. Unlike this, through cryptocurrency, you can avoid the hassle of having to receive and convert at different stages. This pays you according to a standard payment scale instead of the many mental calculations.

There is no delay in receiving payments due to you or sending payments due to you, rather than the necessary conversion. There are also no fees to pay, which keeps the original amount as is and makes it easier and cheaper to make these exchanges and exchanges. It saves money, time and calculations, which paves the way for your approach to be available for servicing elsewhere.

## EASE AND CONVENIENCE

SINCE YOU CAN DECIDE what works as a shortcut and what is not a function at all, it is very convenient and easy for you to use a custom wallet. Multiple cryptocurrencies can also be managed very easily because you can prioritize the functions you want. You decide how important it is to generate statements and what colors make the graphics stand out.

This customization also allows you to choose the graphical interface you want users to access. It is critical in deciding how user-friendly and bold the application is. It increases user interaction on the platform while increasing user satisfaction and is an impetus for more people to join. It also helps you focus your attention span and make appropriate modifications.

## SECURITY AND ASSURANCE

MANY PEOPLE FEEL insecure about using cryptocurrencies even today because of how little they really know about the protocols. To be sure of the efforts that are made to make them for your protection, you must be dependent and trust the provider. In turn, it is the responsibility of the application or website offering the wallet to break it down for them.

. . .

IN ADDITION TO BEING UNAWARE, people are also afraid of being hacked by those who are aware. This is a valid reason to be afraid of fraud, as history shows that people's carelessness leads them to commit fraud. Sending checks, legal warnings and receipts can help them be aware of all legitimate transactions at all times.

RELIABLE and robust

With a reliable infrastructure, Blockchain-based cryptocurrency wallets help people make easy transactions. They have the same interface everywhere and are synchronized with data that is then replicated in the same way across the access area. This reliability and uniformity works best when the exact outcome is known, i.e. with customized wallets.

THE CHANCES of transactions collapsing with Blockchain technology are extremely rare. This increases authenticity. Also, a personalized wallet helps prevent fraud and hacking possibilities with increased protection due to transparency and the need for an algorithm. This makes it resilient and its use becomes more reliable.

Cryptocurrency wallets are like the normal wallets we often use in real life, but the only difference is that they can only store virtual coins. Nowadays, everyone wants to launch their own cryptocurrency with their own brand, so obviously the need for a crypto wallet will be in demand now and also in the future.

A CRYPTO WALLET is like your own bank.

Whatever the business, the core functionality of crypto wallets will never change. Every Blockchain application will require a wallet to store its digital assets, mainly exchange or trading platforms.

The importance of Crypto Wallet in Exchange platforms In general, cryptocurrency exchange platforms are used to exchange cryptocurrencies. So, obviously, an exchange website must require a secure storage where traders can store, buy, sell and transact with their cryptocurrencies. Without a wallet integration, it is impossible to run a successful exchange platform.

So, to start a business based on cryptocurrency exchange, your first requirement will be a secure crypto wallet.

The main purpose behind the creation of decentralized currencies or cryptocurrencies is to give the masses the power to control and manage their own money. So you might ask yourself, "and, don't I have full control of my money?". Since the money we deposit in banks is generally used to lend to others, we technically don't have full control over our "own" money.

WHAT WE OWN IS SIMPLY a promissory note or a promise from the bank to pay us our money. It may sound absurd, but our current monetary system enjoys many fundamental flaws that most of us miss.

CRYPTOCURRENCIES OFFER the power to have absolute and total control over our money.

AND AS CRYPTOCURRENCIES have increased in value, it is vital to have your own cryptocurrency wallet to store and manage your coins.

## WHAT IS A CRYPTO WALLET?

SIMPLIFIED DEFINITION:

.  .  .

IT IS a software program that stores digital currencies.


TECHNICAL DEFINITION:


IT IS a software program that stores your public and private keys, which come in pairs, allowing you to send and receive coins through the Blockchain, as well as monitor your balance.


## HOW DOES IT WORK?

First of all, digital wallets are quite different compared to your physical wallet. Instead of storing money, digital wallets store public and private keys.


PRIVATE KEYS ARE like your PIN number to access your bank account, while public keys are similar to your bank account number. When you send electronic money, you are sending Value in the form of a transaction, transferring ownership of your currency to the recipient.


IN ORDER for the recipient to spend this newly transferred money, your private keys must match the recipient's public address.

Ownership of your private keys gives him full control over the funds associated with your corresponding public keys. This is why it is vital to make sure you keep your private keys hidden in secret so that only you know your private access keys.

If anyone else gets hold of your private keys, they will have control over your coins. It is also equally important to have a backup copy of your private keys, to protect you from accidental loss. You could also lose your funds if you cannot recover your lost private keys.

A WHOLE SET of nurtured elements of vital importance to take into account for those who, like you and me, are starting out in the world of cryptocurrencies and the safe and reliable management of our funds and electronic money.

FINALLY, and on wallets; it is true that, as you can probably realize for yourself, the list offers little variety: cold wallets dominate it, with exchange-based DOGE storage in second place. However, this makes sense for a couple of reasons.

FIRST, Dogecoin is quite popular; and precisely because of its popularity, many cold wallets support the coin without any problems. Granted that hardware cryptographic storage will always be "the way to go" when it comes to security, it's no wonder then that the cold wallet presence is so dominant in our list of the top 10 wallets that support Dogecoin.

THAT SAID, however, there is also the convenience aspect to consider. Not everyone may be a long-term DOGE investor who is willing to accumulate coins for years to come. Some people may prefer to take the active trading route; in a situation like this, using the services of a cold wallet can be a bit cumbersome and time-consuming.

HERE, hot wallets are preferable. This is especially true with exchange-based Dogecoin wallets: they allow you to keep your coins in a secure environment, assuming you are using the services of a top-tier crypto exchange, that is; and also exchange them anywhere.

It is important to know how to discern and choose according to our most honest needs and true requirements, to give optimal utility to a practical, functional and user-friendly resource that fulfills the purposes, ensuring the handling of our safely, quietly and reliably.

# FOUR

# DOGECOIN MINING AND WHY YOU SHOULD PAY ATTENTION TO IT

With thousands of cryptocurrencies to choose from, the world of digital currencies can be quite overwhelming.

For some, one may choose to get involved with cryptocurrencies through Dogecoin mining.

## WHY?

Maybe it's that cuddly, fluffy Shiba Inu face you see everywhere. Or you may have heard that Dogecoin, surprisingly, considering it was created as a joke, has generally held its value over time.

. . .

LIKE BITCOIN, Dogecoin has seen the rise of ASICs, or application-specific integrated circuits, which is a fancy way of saying devices built specifically for mining. Although DOGE's mining algorithm, Scrypt, was originally designed to be ASIC-resistant, ASIC manufacturers eventually found a way around it.

THE INTRODUCTION OF ASICS, which are much more powerful than home computers, at least for mining purposes, has made DOGE mining much more difficult for the average individual, as those using CPUs (computer processing units) and GPUs (graphics processing units) now have to compete with ASIC miners.

IN ADDITION to the rise of ASICs, the introduction of merged mining, the ability to mine DOGE and other cryptocurrencies, has also made Dogecoin mining more difficult. Prior to the addition of merged mining support, some members of the DOGE community were concerned that a small handful of powerful groups dominated Dogecoin mining.

THIS MEANT that those powerful few could launch a 51% attack. In other words, by using the majority (51%) of the hashrate or mining power of the network, these powerful mining groups could change Dogecoin and its Blockchain, or transaction log, completely.

TO COUNTER THIS, Dogecoin developers introduced AuXPoW (Auxiliary-Proof-Of-Work), or Auxiliary Proof-of-Work.

AUXPOW   (AUXILIARY-PROOF-OF-WORK)   ALLOWS miners of other cryptocurrencies to also mine DOGE (merged mining). While this had an effect on the wider distribution of the DOGE hashrate, it also caused the difficulty of mining Dogecoin to skyrocket, making mining more difficult.

FINALLY, due to regularly scheduled decreases in the DOGE block reward, how many Dogecoins are created with each new block on the blockchain, there is less DOGE for miners. This can create downward pressure on miners' profitability unless the price of 1 DOGE can compensate for the lower block rewards.

BECAUSE OF ALL THESE changes in the Dogecoin mining ecosystem over the years, trying to mine Dogecoin on your own with just a CPU or GPU is probably not worth it in terms of profit. However, you may still be able to mine somewhat efficiently if you join a mining pool, but probably only with ASIC mining, which is more expensive.

MINING POOLS ARE groups of miners who join together to combine their hashrate or mining power. By "pooling" together, mining pools have a higher overall hashrate, which means they have a higher probability of earning block rewards. Earnings are divided proportionally among group members, and while payouts may be lower for each individual member, they are generally more consistent than those of solo miners.

Solo miners, as the name implies, are solo miners by themselves. Solo miners keep the mining rewards they earn. However, unless the solo miner has a lot of hash power, their chances of earning block rewards are small. Therefore, their payouts are not made as often or at all.

As mentioned, it is not worth mining DOGE alone with only one CPU or GPU. The exception would be if you are mining with

ASIC(s). But even then it is better to join a group unless you are some sort of DOGE mining ASIC kingpin with a bunch of ASICs.

MINING IS the way a proof-of-work cryptocurrency network allows new coins to enter circulation. To make it work, several computers called "miners" compete to solve a computational puzzle, which involves verifying transactions in a new block and adding them to the main chain. For their efforts, miners get a reward in the form of new coins.

THE MINING PROCESS is fundamental to maintaining network security and enhances decentralization, key aspects of Blockchain technology. But cryptocurrency mining is becoming competitive as more people seek to join the venture. Below, we'll take a brief look at how to profitably mine Dogecoin.

SETTING up a Dogecoin wallet

THE FIRST STEP to mining Dogecoin is to set up a wallet, which is where you will receive the mining reward. Strive to find a secure wallet, preferably hardware wallets that allow you to keep your cryptographic keys offline. Otherwise, a highly secure software wallet will be of great help.

Join a mining group.

TO MINE DOGECOIN PROFITABLY, you need the right equipment and then join a mining group. The reason this is important is that you may not mine any blocks if you go it alone, given the higher difficulty and hash rate requirements. A group will allow you to use the power of many to easily achieve the goal of profit.

## START MINING

ONCE YOU HAVE your mining setup ready, it's time to start mining Dogecoin. However, before you start, make sure everything is set up properly and correctly to avoid possible mishaps along the way. For the hardware, check aspects such as backup power and cooling system, something of vital importance. On a very timely note, make sure it is legal to mine cryptocurrencies in your country.

### WHAT IS NEEDED **to start mining Dogecoin today?**

TO START MINING DOGE right away, you must have set up your own Dogecoin wallet, have the right hardware and software or buy a cloud mining contract. Properly follow each step to safely and simply mine one of the most attractive virtual currencies in the crypto network of the year 2021, which becomes more and more popular thanks to Elon Musk's posts on his social network Twitter about the meme coin: Dogecoin.

### POPULAR HARDWARE **and mining equipment for Dogecoin.**

MINING most popular digital currencies has moved on from CPU usage, and that also applies to Dogecoin. You can mine DOGE using a GPU mining rig. However, the most popular hardware for mining

Dogecoin today is an Application Specific Integrated Circuit (ASIC) device.

THE UNDERLYING DYNAMIC IN MINING, whether it is Dogecoin's Scrypt or another algorithm, is that the hardware devices or platforms that have the most computing power have the greatest chance of mining the next block and getting the reward.

AS THIS IS BECOMING MORE and more defined with the growing popularity of DOGE, getting an ASIC with a good enough hash rate is the first step. Of course, its profitability will still largely depend on other factors, including electricity consumption, efficiency and the price of Dogecoin.

YOU CAN PURCHASE a Dogecoin miner from the manufacturer or any of the various outlets in the market. Remember to do your due diligence before purchasing the platform, including how long it may take before you get a return on investment (ROI).

Below, we introduce you to three main ASIC miners for Dogecoin:

- BITMAIN ANTMINER L3 + The Antiminer L3 +.

E is an ASIC miner from global mining hardware giant Bitmain. The miner comes with a decent hash rate of 504MH/s with a power consumption of 800W and an efficiency of 1.6J/MH at the wall. You can mine DOGE with this miner, as well as other Scrypt-based cryptocurrencies, including Litecoin.

- BW L21 SCRYPT Miner

. . .

THE BW L21 was released January 2018, owned by BW.com. This Scrypt ASIC Miner offers 550 MH/s with a power consumption of 950W and an output efficiency of 1,727j/Mh. This is one of the most powerful ASIC miners for Dogecoin.

## - FUSIONSILICON X6 MINER

THE X6 MINER is an ASIC miner from FusionSilicon released in August 2018. It supports the Scrypt algorithm and is therefore ideal for Dogecoin among other Scrypt-based coins. X6 Miner has a hash rate of 860Mh/s, a power consumption of 1079W and an efficiency of 1,255j/Mh.

## SOFTWARE

BEFORE YOU START MINING CRYPTOCURRENCIES, you need software integration with your hardware. If you decide to mine with an ASIC, you may find it pre-installed with the mining software. However, in case you assemble or purchase a GPU mining rig, you need to download and install the software.

YOU SHOULD MAKE sure to use the software that best suits the type of mining hardware you have. Note also that there are desktop and mobile versions. With the former, you have it on your desktop device and can only access it on that device, while a mobile version allows you to mine on the go.

. . .

## WHAT IS **the software used to mine Dogecoin?**

THE MOST POPULAR mining software you can check out to mine Dogecoin is CGMiner. CGMiner v3.7.2 is a command line interface (CLI) software product that you can easily install and customize according to your configuration. You can also check out MultiMiner and EasyMiner for ASIC hardware and CudaMiner for GPU mining hardware.

Mining Dogecoin with a personal computer Technically, this is something you could try, as Dogecoin mining needs relatively less computing power before the price explosion put it on the map and attracted more hashrate and thus will increase the difficulty.

TODAY, mining Dogecoin with your PC is not a mode through which you can undertake if you really want to make money with it. The simple reason, as noted above, is that you will need a lot more computing power than your own CPU can handle.

AGAIN, if you try this, your computer will quickly overheat and is likely to be damaged. As such, you can only use GPUs or ASICs, and even with the former, you may need a platform comprising 4 or more graphics cards of the best brands and quality.

TECHNICAL KNOWLEDGE NEEDED to mine Dogecoin As you prepare to start mining Dogecoin, you may need to understand some technical terms that apply to the industry. Technical knowledge will help you understand the whole idea of mining.

.  .  .

ALGORITHM IS a set of rules that enables mining, which implies transaction security and Blockchain. Mining algorithms vary and it is good to know which one applies to the currency you want to mine.

IN SIMPLE TERMS let's understand Blockchain as a chain of blocks, referring to the series of data blocks aggregated one after another in a distributed ledger. The blocks must be valid and contain hashes of all transaction data. Miners only get their reward once a block is verified and added to the ledger.

THE HASH RATE is the amount of computing power required to mine new coins. The higher the hash rate, the higher the chances of getting a block. The hash rate is also the total computing power of all miners protecting the network.

THE HIGHER THE HASH RATE, the more difficult it will be to execute a 51% attack.

WHEN WE TALK about Block Time, we mean the time it takes for a miner to find a new block, verify transactions and add it to the blockchain. It is also called block generation time. Dogecoin has a block time of 1 minute, while Litecoin is 2.5 minutes and Bitcoin is 10 minutes.

MINING DIFFICULTY IS the measure of how difficult it is for miners to obtain a new block. It often increases or decreases depending on the number of miners on the network. The difficulty setting ensures that the average block time remains around the coded duration.

. . .

WHEN REFERRING TO MINING FEES, we focus on that small fee a user pays to have their transactions processed on the network. These mining fees are part of a miner's Block Reward.

THE BLOCK REWARD is the reward each miner or group gets for each block they mine and add to the blockchain. It includes the new coins (10,000 DOGE) and transaction/mining fees.

AND FINALLY THE MINING PROFITABILITY. Calculation of potential returns when all mining costs have been taken into account. Miners become profitable when the price of mined coins exceeds the total cost of mining.

IN ADDITION to individual or stand-alone mining, you have the option of joining a Dogecoin mining group. Mining groups combine or pool many miners, "pooling" the hashing power to mine as a single unit. In this way, miners can compete against large farms for the block reward.

A MINING GROUP will reduce the time it would take you to mine a single block, which means you are likely to become profitable faster with a group than as a private miner with a limited budget.

THE MINING GROUP you join should be compatible with Dogecoin's Scrypt algorithm.
Here are two of the most popular ones for this cryptocurrency:

. . .

- PROHASHING:

SUPPORTS SCRYPT, X11, Equihash and SHA-256 and pays in DOGE, not USD, so you have the currency and you can do "hold".

- MULTIPOOL:

HERE YOU CAN DO COMBINED DOGE and Litecoin mining.

DOGECOIN MINING in the cloud is another option you may well consider. Cloud mining allows you to start mining by simply renting the hashing power of one of the data centers.

THIS IS hands-free mining and does not require you to have any hardware or commit time to monitor the equipment. All you have to do is purchase a mining contract, usually monthly or yearly, and pay the appropriate fees that allow you that right. The data center will use your hash rate to mine Dogecoin and pay you a portion of the reward.

REMEMBER that to start mining Dogecoin in the cloud, you need to set up a wallet and find a reputable mining group that offers cloud contracts. Nice Hash and Genesis Mining are the two best options for Scrypt-based coins.

PROS AND CONS **of cloud mining.**

.  .  .

**Pros**

- CHEAPER THAN HARDWARE SETUPS.

- PASSIVE MINING.

- NO NEED TO master technical aspects and terms.

- CAN MINE ANY COIN.

- CONSISTENT REWARD PAYOUT.

CONS

- RISK OF SHADY CONTRACTS.

- LOCKED CONTRACT WITH A FIXED RATE, even if the price drops during the contract.

HOW PROFITABLE CAN **Dogecoin mining be for us?**

WHEN JACKSON PALMER and Billy Markus developed Doge-coin, they thought of it as a 'joke'. They even had the cryptocurrency logo as a Shiba Inu dog, they even seek to discourage serious miners by making the mining reward a random figure. This part meant that a miner could earn anywhere from zero (o) to thousands of DOGE per block.

BUT THAT HAS SINCE CHANGED, with the increased use of Dogecoin making it a coin that really achieves value and importance.

Whether you do your own mining or are part of a mining group, you must first calculate the potential profitability of the coin before proceeding. From this, the important thing is to keep mining expenses below total mining costs.

HERE IS what you need to have to take such an important step:

- MINER'S COST

- HASH RATE VALUE

- ELECTRICITY COST per kWh

- DIFFICULTY.

- POOL RATES

- Dogecoin Price

. . .

IF YOU ACCESS a good Dogecoin mining calculator, you can easily and quickly check the mining profitability of various hardware devices. Most mining calculators also have a list of the best hardware machines, so you can examine as many as possible, focusing on hash rate value, power usage and efficiency.

Suppose you are looking at a Scrypt miner that costs $209.00 and has a hash rate of 540MH/sy, this consumes 800W at 0.05kWh.

If the mining difficulty is 2,818,632.16 you would pay a 1% group rate and earn 10,000.00 DOGE as a block reward at the same time the Dogecoin price is $0.0566 (Example), so this is how profitable it can be.

The daily income would be $2.20 and once you deduct the daily costs, the profit would be reduced to around $1.22.

At this rate, you would reach ROI in 171 days just mining. But finding a block, at this hash rate, would take 238 days. So, your best option is to join a mining group and get the shared payout, with large groups likely to solve a block every day.


WHAT TO DO after mining Dogecoin


NOW, you need to decide whether you will sell the DOGE right away or keep it in your wallet and keep it as a long-term investment. Let's explain these decisions.


SELLING Dogecoin would probably be your first decision if you are looking to make immediate profits. If so, consider two ways to sell the mined DOGE.

Through a cryptocurrency exchange you can sell DOGE, this is the easiest way and you just need to set up an account to proceed. Once set up, you can sell at any time, but you must be very careful of additional costs in fees, as well as price fluctuations.

Through a peer-to-peer platform, the well-known Peer-To-Peer (P2P) marketplace, is also another option for selling your coins. On these platforms, sellers connect directly with buyers and negotiate the terms of the transaction. Once you both agree, you will receive payment and then send the DOGE to the buyer's wallet address.

IF, on the other hand, your desire is to store and hold your mined Dogecoin coins in a secure wallet for the long term, then a popular strategy in crypto circles known as holding would suit you just fine.

THIS SIMPLY MEANS HOLDING the coin for the long term, with the conviction that the coin is undervalued at the current time. If you decide to hold, then make sure to store your DOGE in a reliable wallet, taking as a reference one of the ones mentioned in our previous chapter and below we mention:

- LEDGER NANO S

- KEEP KEY

- Jaxx

- COINOMI

- Dogecoin Wallet

. . .

IN ADDITION TO THEM, you have Coinbase, CoolWallet S and Ledger.

## HOW TO MINE **Dogecoin with GPU**

UNFORTUNATELY, these are the days of ASICs and it probably won't be profitable unless you have a ton of GPUs. Even then, simply buying ASICs would be a better investment for your money.

STILL, if you want to give it a try anyway, maybe to waste your time or get a feel for what DOGE mining is like, you have a few options.

First, set up a GPU mining platform or use whatever GPU your computer currently has.

THEN DOWNLOAD CUDAMiner or CGMiner depending on the type of graphics card you have (CUDA for Nvidia and CG for AMD).

For either program, you will need the following:

- STRATUM ADDRESS and port number to connect to:

STRATUM IS A COIN MINING PROTOCOL, and you can think of a Stratum address as a website address. But instead of connecting to a website, it connects to a mining group.

- YOUR WORKER NAME:

. . .

CREATED on the mining group site.

\- YOUR WORKER PASSWORD:

CREATED on the mining group site, different from your user password for the site.

\- YOUR USERNAME:

FOR THE MINING GROUP SITE.

## HOW TO MINE **Dogecoin with CPU**

IF GPU DOGECOIN mining is not viable, you can forget about CPU mining, at least when it comes to profit. It will probably just make your CPU overheat, which can damage it and reduce its lifespan.

HOWEVER, if you want to play anyway, what you need is to download CPUMiner and have the settings listed above with strat address, port number, worker name, worker password, group site username, perfectly enabled.

## HOW TO MINE **Dogecoin on Android**

· · ·

WHILE IT MAY SOUND cool to be able to mine DOGE with your phone, unfortunately it's not possible. Phones aren't even close to being powerful enough to mine Dogecoin. What you could do is check out the fun Android game Dogeminer.

## HOW TO MINE **Dogecoin on Mac**

IF YOU WANT to mine Dogecoin on your Mac, it probably won't be possible unless you have an amazing GPU. Even then, don't expect it to be profitable, as ASICs will offer stiff competition. Also, don't try this on your Mac, as it will overheat too much, which could cause physical damage and even definitely reduce the lifespan of your device.

ANYWAY, if you still want to get started, follow the instructions in the "How to mine Dogecoin with GPU" section or the "How to mine Dogecoin with CPU" section.

How to mine Dogecoin solo As you may have noticed, mining Dogecoin is somewhat difficult, even with a mining group. The only way to really mine Dogecoin profitably is if you have a Dogecoin mining farm somewhere with a lot of ASIC devices in a place where electricity is very cheap or even free.

OTHERWISE, you run the risk of waiting a long time to receive DOGE block rewards. It may be weeks, months, years or never before you mine a DOGE block yourself. Once you do, though, the entire reward is yours, rather than having to share it with a mining group. However, things like electricity costs could affect any profit you make.

. . .

## HOW LONG DOES **it take to mine Dogecoin?**

TECHNICALLY, one block of Dogecoin is mined every minute. However, if you want to know how long it will take you to mine some DOGE, use something like the WhatToMine Dogecoin mining calculator, but keep in mind that it's not perfect. For example, with an Antminer L3 ++, it will probably take you an hour or less to mine 1 DOGE.

We conclude this session, hoping that you now have a basic understanding of how to mine Dogecoin. While it's largely unprofitable for most these days, that depends on your own situation. Not to mention that things could change if, for example, the price of DOGE goes up.

# FIVE

# THE SECRET OF DOGECOIN'S PRICE EVOLUTION: DOGECOIN TO THE MOON

**DOGECOIN**
**TO THE MOON**

Elon Musk and the controversy with the Dogecoin promotion that raised the value of the cryptocurrency to historic values.

AT THE BEGINNING of the year 2021, specifically between January 27 and February 11, in just 15 days; Dogecoin increased its value by more than 1000%, coupled with this, it has experienced a boost of more than 4000% between November 2020 and February 2021. With all this, and what continues to happen with Dogecoin, it seems that this digital currency will soon embark on a journey so powerful that it will reach the moon. What started as a joke, is already beginning to be seen in its important stage of development and maturity.

THE BEGINNING of the year 2021 started favoring in a very particular and interesting way compared to cryptocurrencies, and one of the great beneficiaries in this aspect and most outstanding has been Dogecoin, since, in its specific condition, two highly powerful elements in the internet world have joined together giving color and highlighting Dogecoin. We are referring to nothing more and nothing less than social networks and memes.

It is enough to appreciate what these digital resources represent by themselves and individually and massively through the internet. If we put them together, imagine what they could do for that which began as a satire and which today we know as Dogecoin. There is no doubt that on the web we can find stories worth spreading, and the Dogecoin story could not be isolated, a story that surpassed itself, becoming something true and that never ceases to amaze us.

SINCE THE BIRTH of the Dogecoin and at the time of writing, Dogecoin has reached a market capitalization of 40,024,275,630.00 USD (June 2021).

IF DOGECOIN WERE to become valued at $1 in price, it would easily reach a market capitalization powerful enough to surpass companies such as Boeing, IBM, American Express or Starbucks Coffee. Undoubtedly, Dogecoin has become one of the most profitable assets of 2021, a situation that should be maintained as long as what started it does not lose its validity.

.  .  .

WITH THE HASHTAGS #DOGEDay or #DOGEDay420, social network users considerably boosted the value of the cryptocurrency and its price reached a record high on Tuesday, April 20, 2021, with a market capitalization of over USD 50 billion, after its users on social networks made posts using the tags to fuel a rally of the cryptocurrency inspired by the "doggy meme".

THE 8,000% increase in its price in the first six months of the current year has made Dogecoin, initially launched almost 8 years ago as part of a satirical critique of the frenzy generated by cryptocurrencies, surpass other valuable recognized cryptocurrencies such as Tether, and become the fifth largest worldwide.

DESPITE THE FACT that Dogecoin represents only a fraction of Bitcoin's $1 trillion value, it can be traded on cryptocurrency exchanges and popular trading applications. The logo of the digital currency is represented by the Shiba Inu dog meme.

THE RISE in Dogecoin's price performance represents an interesting convergence, after the Dogecoin price quintupled in the last week to a record high of $0.42 USD, according to CoinMarketCap. Dogecoin, a coin created as a joke for its early cryptocurrency users, whose community found this sort of thing very funny, now represents a new generation of retail investors for whom memes have since become part of a native language.

Dogecoin has been benefited in its price many times by the reactions expressed on the network even by those who have not yet bought it. That detail of placing the face of a dog as its logo, somehow makes it gain fans and followers, who although they do not invest in the coin; they identify with it because of the love, care and affection towards pets. So much so that every day there are countless, to say the least; the memes published in social networks with the face of Kabosu, Atsuko Sato's dog, the image of Dogecoin.

But another great factor, inherent to the crypto world itself, does wonders to give value and prestige to Dogecoin, and that is its presence and acceptance in various areas of the market, in productive sectors of the industry and in business and marketing spaces.

The fact that the currency is valid and accepted to be able to pay for a coffee, says enough. Something like when we give it the trust that fiat money needs so much to be accepted and circulate, well, Dogecoin is gaining more ground. In addition to sympathy and trust, it is gaining support and commercial backing.

FOR THE FIRST days of June 2021, Dogecoin received what we could call praise or praise for two important situations that helped it to quote its value with a significant growth that led it to be located around $0.39 per coin compared to $0.32 in which it was, before Coinbase Pro, one of the most important exchanges located in the United States, announced the incorporation and availability of Dogecoin; announced the incorporation and availability of Dogecoin in its platform, so that interested people could start depositing their Dogecoin tokens in their respective accounts.

DOGECOIN MANAGED to recover more than 20% against this important announcement, in which Coinbase Pro let it know that it would add it to its list of cryptocurrency exchanges, one of the largest and most recognized platforms in the crypto world.

THE ANNOUNCEMENT of this exchange sparked an interest aroused in the cryptocurrency seized by memes, just like the tweets of Elon Musk, CEO of Tesla, who with some frequency and regularity shakes the cryptocurrency markets just by activating his social networks. For this occasion Musk reacted to the Coinbase Pro announcement by reposting an old tweet in which he called the emergence of Dogecoin "inevitable," only to later reignite interest in the coin on social media with another DOGE-based meme.

SOCIAL MEDIA and its impact on the value of Dogecoin

DOGECOIN FOLLOWERS and fans used the hashtags #DOGEDay and #DOGEDay420 to post memes, messages and videos on their social networks on Twitter, Reddit and TikTok, in reference to the April 20 celebration and informal holiday to exalt cannabis, which is marked by stoners and street parties.

LIKE MANY OTHER CRYPTOCURRENCIES, Dogecoin's price is heavily influenced by social media users, including Tesla CEO Elon Musk, whose tweets about the cryptocurrency in February sent its price soaring more than 60%.

With no discussion and nothing to add, Dogecoin has become the cryptocurrency starring in memes and social networks. Born from a meme, it has remained driven mainly by social networks and their millions of memes around the world. For this reason, it is no coincidence that its price remains so high. The community itself, while having fun, invests and increases the price of this asset.

THE CURRENT PRICE of Dogecoin is at $0.31, which is not much lower than the historical maximum of $0.41. Equally it is still five times higher as the April 15 boom was not followed by a dump.

The year-to-date gain is up 524% from March 2021, and up 17,590% from a year ago.

. . .

HOWEVER, it is worth noting that there seems to be a speculative bubble around the price of DOGE, and it would not be surprising if this bubble will burst sooner or later, a currency that was born from a meme and is mainly driven by memes and memes on social networks. Therefore, it is no coincidence that its price remains so high.

Dogecoin prices surged 50% in less than 24 hours after one of the world's richest men, Elon Musk, tweeted a meme of himself and the cryptocurrency's logo in the style of the Disney movie "The Lion King."

WITH JUST A FEW TWEETS, Elon Musk has triggered a run on the market of a little-known cryptocurrency, such as Dogecoin.

According to the website Coinmarketcap.com, a cryptocurrency data provider, the price of Dogecoin rose about 50% to $0.02610 (€0.022), almost 3 cents in less than 24 hours.

TRADING VOLUME also tripled throughout the day as Musk, head of electric automaker Tesla and spacecraft producer SpaceX, had fueled the surge by simply posting the word "DOGE" on Twitter with an image of a moon rocket.

HE THEN WROTE: "Dogecoin is the people's cryptocurrency." "No ups and downs, just DOGE," he added.

WHAT DISTINGUISHES Dogecoin from other computer-derived currencies is that the amount of digital coins that can be generated through "mining" is not limited.

. . .

IN THE GENERATION PROCESS, users contribute computer capacity for transaction encryption. Users are then paid in the corresponding cryptocurrency.

SINCE DOGECOIN'S encryption is simpler, transactions can be processed faster than with Bitcoin or Litecoin.

Dogecoin advertises itself as a decentralized open-source Peer-To-Peer (P2P) digital currency that allows users to easily send money online.

However, analyst Timo Emden of Emden Research warned that it is not sustainable. "For investors, the market environment with Dogecoin resembles going to a casino."

MUSK IS FOLLOWED by more than 45 million people on Twitter, but his social media influence is also driven by his pop icon status.

Neil Wilson, chief analyst at online broker Markets.com, said that "people are literally investing in him and his ideas." The contest for those ideas doesn't matter, according to the expert.

ALTHOUGH MUSK recently promised to take a break from Twitter, beyond making several online comments there that boosted Dogecoin's value, he recently sparked a rally around Bitcoin, its price surging above $38,000 last week after Musk changed his Twitter bio to include "#bitcoin." Within hours, Bitcoin had increased in price to over $38,741.00.

DOGECOIN PRICE RISES after tweets from Elon Musk and Mark Cuban.

·  ·  ·

- "DOGECOIN SOARED on Wednesday after receiving some celebrity endorsements on Twitter."

DOGECOIN'S PRICE has soared 20% in the past 24 hours to 32 cents, according to data from Coin Metrics. The meme-inspired cryptocurrency hit a record high of more than 45 cents earlier this month, sparking fears of a possible bubble in the cryptocurrency market.

Initially started as a joke in 2013, Dogecoin is now the sixth-largest digital currency with a total market value of nearly $42 billion, according to CoinGecko. It takes its name and branding from the meme "DOGE," which depicts a Shiba Inu dog along with nonsense phrases in multicolored text.

IT HAS OFTEN RISEN in price following tweets from Elon Musk. The billionaire CEO of Tesla once called Dogecoin his "favorite" cryptocurrency and "the people's cryptocurrency." Musk is also a bitcoin supporter, as his electric car company has amassed nearly $2.5 billion in cryptocurrencies.

On Wednesday, Musk simply tweeted, "The DOGEfather SNL May 8." This is both a reference to his frequent tweets about Dogecoin, which he says are "meant to be jokes," and Musk's planned appearance on "Saturday Night Live" next week.

A very special magic revolves around the ingenuity, creativity, professionalism and expertise that Elon Musk possesses, but his unique influence on social networks vis-à-vis the crypto market, makes him "The Influencer" number one of the currency. A few characters written and posted generate turbulence in the market, usually triggering the price of Dogecoin to unexpected levels.

· · ·

AND NOT ONLY MUSK, celebrities like Mark Cuban, renowned American businessman, investor, and owner of the Dallas Mavericks NBA team, who is also owner of Landmark Cinemas, and Magnolia Pictures, as well as president of the HDTV Cable TV network AXS TV and who is also well known for his investment and participation in the series "Shark Tank"; has declared and published in favor of Dogecoin, cataloging it in his forecasts as a StableCoin that will surely reach $1.00 in value very soon. Cuban owns an estimated 3,250.00 Dogecoin. For Mark Cuban, investing in Dogecoin turns out to be much better than playing the lottery.

SNOOP DOGG, American musician, composer and rap singer, as well as producer and actor, is also a regular follower and investor in Dogecoin. Last April 20, 2021, as part of the DOGEDay celebration, Snoop dedicated a 45-second video to the cryptocurrency, where he appears traveling, dancing and fighting in an extraterrestrial plane, accompanied by a Shiba Inu, symbol of the currency. Publication that generated positive reactions in his virtual Twitter community @SnoopDogg. Snoop, who in the past had hinted at the possibility of launching his own virtual currency "Dogecoin", is a fervent advocate of Dogecoin. His publications on behalf of Dogecoin are a boost to its value.

ANOTHER RELEVANT FIGURE who is part of the DOGE community is Gene Simmons (Chaim Witz). Musician, composer, singer, music producer, actor, author, entrepreneur and television personality of Jewish-Hungarian descent and Israeli-American nationality and also known as co-founder, bassist and co-leader of the rock band Kiss, has become an investor in Dogecoin.

Simmons self-declared himself "God of Dogecoin", inspired by his song "God Of Thunder". Gene Simmons broke the market by starting as an investor in Dogecoin. In an interview conducted by bitcoin.com, Simmons expressed the following: "I don't think, for a second, that people understand what cryptocurrency is or what it's designed to do. However, it's immediate and allows you to not have to deal with banks, and I like that." Enough, don't you think?

DOGECOIN'S PRICE continues to soar, according to data from Coin Metrics. The meme-inspired cryptocurrency has reached record highs to above 45 cents, sparking fears of a possible bubble in the cryptocurrency market.

Initially started as a joke in 2013, Dogecoin is now the sixth largest digital currency with a total market value of nearly $40 billion, according to CoinGecko. It takes its name and branding from the meme "DOGE," which depicts a Shiba Inu dog along with nonsense phrases in multicolored text.

It has often risen in price following Elon Musk's tweets. The billionaire CEO of Tesla once called Dogecoin his "favorite" cryptocurrency and "the people's cryptocurrency." Musk is also a Bitcoin supporter, as his electric car company has amassed nearly $2.5 billion in cryptocurrencies.

Recently, Musk simply tweeted, "The DOGEfather SNL May 8." This is as much a reference to his frequent tweets about Dogecoin, which he says are "meant to be jokes."

Elon Musk is a very influential character who rocks the cryptoverse and allowed to shake up the crypto market, especially for Dogecoin with a very simple poll on Twitter.

FOLLOWING a simple high-impact query via his social network Twitter @elonmusk, billionaire Elon Musk asked the following question: do you want Tesla to accept DOGE? Referring to the Dogecoin cryptocurrency, a digital currency that Musk has toyed with in recent months. After his question, the price of the coin skyrocketed, as expected; and all to the detriment of other similar currencies such as

Bitcoin or Ethereum, which pay with sharp falls the umpteenth appearance of the founder of Tesla.


THE INTERESTING QUESTION has arisen a few days after labeling the interesting doggy coin as a "hot" crypto, which generated that the price of this virtual currency conceived in memes shuddered after a galloping 700% spike in just one month. Musk, a radical advocate of digital currencies, expressed this comment during a special appearance as a guest and host on the comedy TV magazine "Saturday Night Live".

# SIX

# WHY IS DOGECOIN NOT CONSIDERED A SERIOUS CRYPTOCURRENCY WITHIN THE CRYPTOCURRENCY COMMUNITY?

Tokens related to Dogecoin: Shiba Inu and Akita.

Dogecoin is a peer-to-peer cryptocurrency named after a popular Internet meme. The idea started as a joke, but is quickly becoming serious.

Now, can a joke be taken seriously?

AS WE'RE PRETTY clear by now, back in 2013, Dogecoin was created as a way to poke fun at an industry that took itself too seriously. Now, and after memes, abandonments, neglect and oblivion for many; it is one of the largest cryptocurrencies in the world, before which we wonder how did it get here? Well, somehow and unknowingly, Dogecoin generated a lively community of enthusiasts that from the very first moment and based on its principles began to follow and bet on it, the joker coin.

SINCE 2013, the time of its emergence; Dogecoin has come a long and fruitful way reaching a market value of over $40 billion at its peak in today's cryptocurrency craze. Jackson Palmer, an Adobe employee, couldn't believe the sheer number of altcoins popping up in 2013. As a joke, he sent out a tweet saying he was investing in Dogecoin, a non-existent coin at the time and based on the Shiba Inu dog meme that was popular by then.

Although he tweeted in jest, there were many people who thought he was making a serious and true comment. They said that the industry really needed a lighthearted token that could counter the more controversial coins on offer. That's how Palmer then teamed up with Billy Markus, a programmer, to make Dogecoin a reality.

Let's take a look at this brief historical overview that gives certainty to Dogecoin's presence, existence and permanence.

- DECEMBER 2013: Dogecoin was founded by Jackson Palmer.

- JUNE 2014: Dogecoin Foundation is established to preside over the currency code.

- APRIL 2015: Co-founder Jackson Palmer leaves Dogecoin.

. . .

- JANUARY 2018: Briefly surpasses $2 billion market capitalization.

- MAY 2019: Dogecoin is added to the popular Coinbase wallet.

- MARCH 2020: Elon Musk says Dogecoin is the best cryptocurrency - April 2021: DOGEDay established on April 4

DOGECOIN BECOMES A SERIOUS COIN, and this makes it special Can it be taken seriously?

- SPEED AND COST: It boasts fast transactions and low transaction fees, both of which are essential for widespread adoption.

- UNLIMITED SUPPLY: Originally, the coin had a limit of 100 billion coins, but then it was changed to unlimited supply. That keeps the price relatively stable.

- COMMUNITY: The heart of Dogecoin is its active community. The 100,000+ members on Reddit are famous for being a friendly and welcoming group.

- PHILANTHROPY: That same community is known to rally around good causes. They raised more than $25,000 in Dogecoin to help send the cash-strapped Jamaican bobsled team to the 2014 Olympics. They also partnered with a water charity to raise thousands to improve access to clean water in Kenya.

. . .

SINCE THERE IS an unlimited supply of Dogecoin tokens, the value of a single token is very low compared to other altcoins. That means mining is not very profitable, so there is not much incentive. However, the low reward does not deter Dogecoin enthusiasts. For them, it was never intended to be an investment; it was meant to be a dynamic currency.

THE ADVANTAGE of the endless supply of Dogecoin tokens is that the price remains relatively stable. The disadvantage is that the price usually remains very low. Most people enter the world of cryptocurrencies as an investment. They hope that if they hold on to certain tokens long enough, they can sell them for a profit.

NOT SO WITH DOGECOIN. Since the supply of tokens is high and the price is low, it is not attractive to investors looking to hold their currency. The result is a highly liquid and fluid peer-to-peer digital currency.

WHETHER IT'S a serious coin or not What can you do with Dogecoin?

A KEY USE of Dogecoin is an online tipping system. If you like what someone posted on Dogecoin's Reddit community, you can leave a tip. This is part of what gives the community its friendly reputation and seriousness.

. . .

YOU CAN ALSO MAKE exchanges for other cryptocurrencies on various exchanges, which has made the coin an unlikely means by which people hop from one exchange to another. For something that started as a joke, Dogecoin has established a legitimate and true reputation. Even co-founder Jackson Palmer criticizes the extreme seriousness with which people take it today.

Palmer left in 2015 after scammers fleeced fun-loving members of the Dogecoin community. He said too many people were jumping in with a "get rich quick" mentality, without achieving the coin's purpose. When Dogecoin briefly reached a $2B market cap in January 2018, Palmer remained critical, to which he tweeted, "I think it says a lot about the state of the cryptocurrency space in general that a coin with a dog that hasn't released a software update in over 2 years has a $1B+ market cap."

THAT SAID, the Dogecoin community remains active and loyal. With the ease of acquiring Dogecoin, low trading cost and relatively stable price, it could very well stick around for the future.

Now, why should we take Dogecoin seriously? Dogecoin's rise reflects the power of collective belief and the yearning for a more ideal form of cryptocurrency.

Dogecoin started 2021 on the right foot, a dog-themed cryptocurrency that has recently skyrocketed in value, thanks in part to support from Elon Musk and other celebrities. For a time it was the 10th largest cryptocurrency. Dogecoin ended 2020 at less than half a cent per DOGE, according to CoinDesk's Dogecoin Price Index. It now trades above 0.30 cents per DOGE, which puts its year-to-date returns at around 1,000%.

It may be tempting to dismiss this as a speculative frenzy or just a fluke, but that would be missing the bigger picture. We should take note of Dogecoin's rise, if only because it reflects some of the key stresses of this moment in time.

. . .

REFERRING TO DOGECOIN, with the passage of its brief time in existence, a very fine line prevails between absurdity and seriousness and oddly enough; between mockery and seriousness. Dogecoin literally bears the name of a dog and is represented by a Shiba Inu, something that, incredibly, many do not like. Added to this is the case of rapper Snoop Dogg, who recently renamed himself "Snoop DOGE". If all this sounds laughable, that's because it is, even if his fans don't want to accept it. The creators of Dogecoin intended their creation to be a joke, the joke within the crypto world, but now apparently absurdity is built in and is part of its design.

Today, some of the more serious people in the not always "so serious" crypto industry are upset by the prominence of Dogecoin. Its recent developers are joining efforts to make people see and convince them that the cryptocurrency has real and true technology behind it. The results of this effort are starting to show, as the world is now paying more attention to Dogecoin, from celebrities to ordinary netizens, big companies and entrepreneurs.

With this trend, almost every day there seems to be a new brand or company trying to get in on the action in favor of Dogecoin. Cases like PayPal, Tesla, MasterCard, Harvard, Morgan Stanley and even America's oldest bank BNY Mellon; and so the list continues to grow as the price of Bitcoin has responded accordingly, surpassing $30,000 recently.

Our society is phenomenal. What once seemed like an absurdity to many can become radically very serious. Prior to 2016, much of the world's society, including Obama himself; viewed Donald Trump as a scandalous reality TV star who was seen as having no chance of winning the U.S. presidency. They saw him as a joke, and many still do despite the reality. However, Donald Trump triumphed, won and became the president for four full years of the most powerful nation on the planet.

.  .  .

OBVIOUSLY, this is not the most perfect comparison, and the point of ours is not to compare Dogecoin to Trump. It is simply to accentuate that Dogecoin "teased" to reach a market cap of about $2 billion, and that is a lot of money, real, true and serious money. It also means and means that, if DOGE mania ever breaks out, some people will face very real, serious big losses for not taking "stuff" seriously.

JUST LIKE TRUST and other values, collective belief can trump "fundamentals" How did this happen? How did something that seems patently absurd become undeniably real?

In part, it is because reality seems to be increasingly shaped by collective beliefs, rather than underlying facts.

This collective belief can override more practical concerns. Until recently, Dogecoin was essentially abandoned by developers, with its last major software release occurring two years ago. Others have pointed out that it lacks its own miners, making it vulnerable to attack. Critics will say that DOGE's recent boom is driven entirely by speculation, rather than fundamental value.

Dogecoin is a sentiment-driven asset. But lately, a lot of things feel that way. Value is created from crowd sentiment and fueled by social media. The most obvious example is GameStop, where Redditers joined forces to drive up the price of a stock in a very short time. A more recent example is MarsCoin, which skyrocketed over 1,000% after Musk simply mentioned it on Twitter. The power of credibility, digital impact and social media clout, wielded by Elon Musk, have made Dogecoin, case in point; a fantastic phenomenon of momentum and growth.

"WHAT IS DIFFERENT NOW IS THAT SOCIAL NETWORKS CAN TRANSLATE COLLECTIVE BELIEF INTO COLLECTIVE ACTION AT AN UNPRECEDENTED PACE AND SCALE."

. . .

TEENS REACH dizzying levels of fame on TikTok, fueled by collective fan support and the app's mysterious algorithm. Do those seconds-long videos deserve global recognition? Are these people deserving of fame? Maybe not, maybe yes; but neither is it really relevant. Some are becoming millionaires. This may be harmless, but less so are Internet-driven conspiracy theories that don't have to be based in fact to have real-world consequences. People just have to believe it to be true.

Collective belief has always been a powerful force, but it can't move markets on its own. What is different now is that social networks can translate collective belief into collective action at an unprecedented pace and scale. Celebrities like Musk have been able to leverage their huge fan bases to galvanize people to make concrete moves like buying example DOGE and raising its price.

A product of all this digital and commercial movement, people want decentralization, but it remains out of reach. The idea of collective belief is at the heart of money and therefore crypto culture. Without a shared belief in its value, fiat currency would be little more than paper and metal.

BUT WHILE CENTRAL governments can print money and have an impact on the price, Dogecoin is meant to be free and independent of that monitored system. The price of DOGE, simply put, is determined by how much people are willing to pay for it. In the early days, that was just a few cents. Now, it's almost close to 0.50 cents, which for Dogecoin, is very significant.

DOGECOIN REPRESENTS an ideal of what cryptocurrency was supposed to be. It is truly bizarre and lives outside the financial system. Its founders have effectively left the scene, leaving it in the hands of the community, leaving it free. The big banks want nothing to do with it. It seems safe to say that it will be a while before we see a major headline with Goldman Sachs and Dogecoin, for example.

DOGECOIN HAS CLEARLY GROWN and is gaining respect among a well-weighted number of investors. A very positive thing for widespread adoption and perhaps for the industry as a whole. But the maturation of DOGE has also come with a degree of centralization: large investors (known as whales) enjoy mammoth influence, as do certain mining groups and exchanges.

Musk is a well-known Bitcoin fan and has suggested that Dogecoin should become the "people's cryptocurrency," i.e., a democratic form of money. This taps into the zeitgeist we saw in the GameStop momentum, which was an assertion of the strength of retail investors over large hedge funds. But is GameStop, entertaining as it was in reality, certainly going to alter the balance of power in the financial world?

DEMOCRATIZATION OF FINANCE is hard to achieve. So it should come as no surprise that Dogecoin is not so decentralized after all. Musk recently pointed out that Dogecoin's wealth is too concentrated. This claim was backed up by Coin Metrics, which noted that the top 100 DOGE addresses contain 68% of its total supply, compared to Bitcoin's 13.7%. Put another way, the top 1% of DOGE addresses have 94% of the total supply.

Musk has tried to address this problem by urging large DOGE holders to sell, even offering to pay them money to write off their accounts. But it's hard to escape the irony here. One incredibly wealthy man bid up the price of Dogecoin and then complained about a concentration of power, which he offered to fix himself.

·  ·  ·

DOGECOIN SHOULD BE TAKEN SERIOUSLY, if not literally. Its rise is highlighting tensions that won't go away anytime soon. We should pay attention to them. Otherwise, the joke is on us. It would be us, the community who would play into the irony itself.

Dogecoin is already an important part of the crypto ecosystem, and on a daily basis it is subjected to evidence its relationship, value and capitalization with the most important digital currencies in the world, being part of the Top 10 of the cryptoverse. Given this, there are two curious digital currencies related in image with Dogecoin. We are talking about Shiba Inu and Akita Inu.

Shiba Inu Virtual currency created in August 2020 by Ryoshi, is also a joke coin or meme that was launched as a rival or competition for Dogecoin.

Shiba Inu has been in the news and newsworthy for two simple reasons. Recently, Tesla founder Elon Musk tweeted saying that he would like to have a Shiba puppy which excited the cryptocurrency market and prices increased by 300%.

SHIBA INU COIN prices fell about 40% after 27-year-old Russian-Canadian billionaire Vitalik Buterin, the creator of Ethereum, donated 50 billion Shiba Inu coins to India's Covid Crypto Relief Fund, managed by Indian crypto-entrepreneur Sandeep Nailwal.

THE OWNER of Shiba Inu is "someone" named or known by the pseudonym Ryoshi, although no one knows this person's real name. The meme coin is named after the Japanese dog breed Shiba Inu. Incidentally, Shiba Inu had claimed to be the "Dogecoin Killer" when it was launched in August 2020 and is seen as a rival to Dogecoin. Shiba Inu's mascot is based on Shiba's puppy and looks quite similar to Dogecoin's. The platform and model are also based on Dogecoin.

· · ·

HOW DIFFERENT DOES Shiba Inu turn out to be in this field from its supposed rival?

DOGECOIN HAS BEEN DEVELOPED USING the same technology as Bitcoin. Shiba Inu tokens are powered by Ethereum. Expendable tokens like Shiba Inu are ERC-20 tokens and non-fungible tokens (NFT) use the ERC-721 token standard of the Ethereum platform.

THE SHIB TOKEN is our first token and allows users to hold billions or even billions of them, mentions the official website. More additions are coming according to the Shiba Inu website. The creators plan to launch Bone Dogecoin Killer, the next coin in the future.

IN INDIA, it is possible to exchange Shiba Inu digital currency on WazirX. WazirX mistakenly listed it at Rs 3 and the company clarified that an incorrect configuration caused the listing to have a higher value. After it was discovered, prices plummeted to $0.0015 levels.

OTHER PLATFORMS such as Uniswap and the web version of CoinDCX have also listed Shiba Inu tokens. The Decentralized Exchange (DEX) Uniswap, on the Ethereum network also allows buying and selling cryptocurrencies for ETH and other Ethereum-based tokens. These coins cannot be bought in Indian rupees (INR), only in USDT / BUSD.

ACCORDING TO SATHVIK VISHWANATH, CEO and co-founder of Unocoin, Dogecoin started as a meme coin and established itself to some extent as a viable means of making online payments even for smaller transactions where well-known coins like Bitcoin and Ether failed. Miserably due to their high transaction fees that increased due to their own popularity.

On the other hand, Vishwanath said, the world still needs an experimental meme currency and we have Shiba INU filling that void.

"Shiba INU seems to be increasing in price more due to buzz than utility, while DOGE seems to have found a use case on the ground," added Sathvik Vishwanath, CEO and co-founder of Unocoin.

There is a risk factor between Shiba Inu and Dogecoin and that is that they are meme coins, so they can be extremely volatile at times.

IN ADDITION, the most important risk of investing in any cryptocurrency is that they are not regulated nor do they have a legal body to oversee their operations. On occasion, the central bank has issued several warnings to cryptocurrency traders about possible losses due to adverse developments.

According to experts, cryptocurrency exchange platforms such as Coinbase, Robinhood and Kraken allow buying Dogecoin. To buy Dogecoin on these platforms, investors must download a cryptocurrency wallet.

IN ADDITION, users can also mine one Dogecoin. Those who have a powerful computer setup can process other Dogecoin transactions and get these coins as payments.

To reiterate, and it is important to keep in mind that users can exchange Shiba Inu digital coins on WazirX as well as on the Uniswap platform and the web version of CoinDCX.

· · ·

UNISWAP IS a decentralized Exchange (DEX) on the Ethereum network that allows you to buy and sell cryptocurrencies for ETH and other Ethereum-based tokens. Remember, Shiba Inu cannot be exchanged or bought in Indian Rupees (INR) only in USDT / BUSD.

Given these aspects, according to Ashish Singhal, CEO and co-founder of CoinSwitch Kuber; investors should conduct thorough research on the fundamentals of the coin and delve into the use case for it.

"Factors such as risk management should also be taken into account. That said, one should only put in the amount that is okay to lose in these currencies." Singhal.

Akita Inu

SELF-DUBBED DOGECOIN'S LITTLE BROTHER, it is a decentralized community-driven experiment. No founders, no team tokens. The purpose of this group is to assign skills within the community to appropriate roles in Akita's development and collec-tively agree on decisions for Akita's future.

Like cryptocurrencies, memes were born on the Internet and have traveled from the fringes to the mainstream. They are used to drive cryptocurrency adoption, signal bullish or bearish movements in certain assets or coins by traders and even increase the value of tokens.

Akita Blocked 50% of the total supply to Uniswap and threw away the keys. The remaining 50% was burned to Vitalik Buterin. There is no greatness without a vulnerable point and as long as Buterin represents no nuisance, AKITA will grow, survive and develop. His people believe and are sure that everyone should have equal opportunities to own Akita, there is no equipment token.

Everyone has to buy on the open market, this means that developers have no more ownership rights than anyone else in the world.

Akita Inu is a token, a 100% decentralized community experiment and claims that half of the tokens were sent to Vitalik Buterin and the other half were locked in a Uniswap group and the keys burned. It's just like Shiba Inu, but with different tokenmetrics and inspired by Elon Musk and Dogecoin.

THE AKITA TOKEN is now available on the Ethereum mainnet. The token address for AKITA is 0x3301ee63fb29f863f2333b-d446666acb46cd8323e6.

If you are going to buy Akita, be careful not to buy any other token with a different smart contract than this one, as it can be very easily counterfeited. We strongly recommend being vigilant and safe throughout the launch. Don't let the excitement get the better of you. Just make sure you have enough ETH in your wallet to cover the transaction fees.

You will first need to purchase one of the major cryptocurrencies, usually Bitcoin (BTC), Ethereum (ETH), Tether (USDT), Binance (BNB) to acquire Akita.

Launched just 5 months ago, Akita Inu is a humble ERC 20 token with bold results so far. Originally found on Uniswap, as of mid-April 2021 it has been added to multiple exchanges including MXC, HotBit, Poloniex and more for a total of 7 platforms and a new one with BKEX.

THIS RAPID ADOPTION was made possible with several days of trading volume of over $200,000,000.00 and resulted in trending status on CoinMarketCap and CEX.

Akita Inu is being built exclusively with the help of community feedback. A truly democratized project.

Recently, more than 15,000 new investors now hold this token and another 22,000 have joined their project on Telegram, where followers will start to give special shape to this plan.

NEW COMMUNITY IDEAS being adopted by the project include a token burning, betting to enable passive income on the holder's dormant currency, and finally the development of its own decentralized social network comparable to Twitter, where users will be able to interact with each other. The function to tip Akita to show your support is enabled. All this will be possible with a partnership with Polarfox.

THE TEAM IS ALSO days away from a new Akita website launch that beautifully illustrates the roadmap to come.

IN THE EARLY days of a new project, it is always easy to claim that something new will be comparable to something else, which is more proven. We do not intend to make such a comparison in this article. Rather, the core belief of the token is a much more intriguing comparison that should be made as to why Akita Inu could be the next Dogecoin: The Power of Community.

FIRST, let's look at why Dogecoin became the #6 coin on CoinMarketCap. It was created in 2013 as a peer-to-peer P2P (Peer-To-Peer) digital currency and even in the early days, it was considered a comedic coin. After all, its logo is a cartoon of a dog. But it was this humor that was able to penetrate deep into the Internet and immediately became a force and a real competitor, even compared to Bitcoin. The community grew around the idea that, despite its comical nature, what if our little furry friend could be the benchmark cryptocurrency in the market, chasing traditional financial institutions?

. . .

OVER TIME, the power of Dogecoin's ability to compete became more difficult under the scrutiny of cryptocurrencies that needed a purpose. Fear of fraudulent coins and obviously a very unregulated market kept Dogecoin at a very low price. That is, until the winter boom of 2017 and 2018. DOGE's price broke a penny. Although later in 2018, the market collapsed again in what looked like a bear market for the entire industry, including Bitcoin.

But the power of the DOGE community stayed with Dogecoin. The interesting thing about the Reddits forums at the time is that the sentiment was not supportive of DOGE. Not because people thought it would generate profits, but rather because of a desire to put a middle finger on the financial world. It was this common belief that kept people interested and willing to continue to support something that had no practical purpose. It was the power of the community that organically created its own purpose.

## WHY CREATE AN AKITA COMMUNITY?

FAST FORWARD TO 2020 and 2021. At this point, financial institutions have entered the cryptocurrency space and Bitcoin is at record highs. Financial institution participation and more people than ever are looking to invest in cryptocurrencies as projects like Akita Inu are ripe for the picking. Both old and new cryptocurrency investors see how far Dogecoin has come and many of the same sentiments of playful anti-establishment investors will be looking for the next Dogecoin.

In late 2020 and early 2021, we saw people on Reddit nearly bankrupt one of the world's largest hedge funds for shorting Gamestop stock. A collective group of average individuals pulled off one of the most important financial moves of the last century.

They realized one thing: the power of community.

Akita Inu is an interesting project that realizes the power of community as well, and it should be mentioned that their logo is also a dog. An Akita Inu to be specific, which is a Japanese bear hunting dog. A fitting name for a cryptocurrency that is trying to fight future bear markets with the power of the community.

THERE ARE CURRENTLY OVER 20,000 members in the Akita network on the social networking platform Telegram @akitatoken, and 2,000 to 5,000 active members online at any given time as of April 18, 2021.

ON ETHERSCAN, there are already 11,000 holders of the coin and the number seems to be climbing at a rapid pace as more people learn about the affordable price of Akita Inu. What should get investors excited about this is that it is still very new and the foundations of a strong and robust community are already taking shape.

SO, in comparing Akita Inu and Dogecoin, there is one factor that is very similar, a factor that is really the make or break element here, in a word: Community.

Looking at the basic foundation upon which Akita Inu has been built and the amount of engagement within the community itself, there is no reason why momentum cannot continue and even be a strong bull during a bear market due to long-term affordability.

HOWEVER, the mindset of the community is also important and will be something to consider.

• • •

IS the community just hoping for quick wins? Or does the community understand the long term game, that they have an opportunity in years, not months or weeks?

WILL they attract Dogecoin supporters with an attitude of rebellion towards financial institutions while also balancing and promoting a fun and playful environment?

ONLY TIME WILL TELL how this project will evolve, but from its creation, Akita Inu seems poised to make a name for itself in the marketplace in the coming years. For those interested in learning a little more, we invite you to check out the messages anchored in their active Telegram group. There, you'll find the roadmap and get updates on where this community will grow.

DOGECOIN: The world's most valuable crypto joke The cryptocurrency has outperformed all others over the past year and is now valued at $70 billion. Based on a meme, it has ironically proven to be quite responsive to jokes, as revealed in a recent Elon Musk joke.

It only took one joke to send the value of Dogecoin, one of the world's most popular cryptocurrencies, plummeting 30%.

THE CRYPTOCURRENCY, which began as a joke on social media eight years ago, lost more than a third of its price after Elon Musk, one of the world's richest men and Dogecoin's most prominent supporter, called the digital currency a "hustle" during his appearance on the sketch comedy television show Saturday Night Live on May 8, 2021.

·  ·  ·

THE SHARP DROP was an anti-climax to a week-long buildup by Dogecoin enthusiasts in the run-up to Musk's guest host appearance on the popular show. Dogecoin's price had surged to a record high before the show aired, as fans organized viewing parties in anticipation of a big boost for the cryptocurrency after Musk's appearance.

"MUSK IS PROBABLY happy to jump on the joke of what is a meme currency, but investors are probably feeling real pain now," said Justin d'Anethan, Hong Kong-based head of exchange sales at Diginex, a digital asset exchange.

Supply is essentially unlimited for Dogecoin and therefore unsustainable in the long run. It is a question of who will sell first and who will keep the exchanges.

INTEREST IN CRYPTOCURRENCIES has surged over the past year, pushing the value of all digital currencies to more than $2.3 trillion, backed by trillions of dollars in stimulus from governments and central banks and the backing of some institutional investors.

While Bitcoin, the most valued cryptocurrency by some distance, has hogged much of the limelight and posted record rallies, it is the so-called altcoins such as Ethereum and Dogecoin that have taken over in recent days.

## THE RISING **popularity of Dogecoin**

THERE IS no easy explanation behind the rising prices of Dogecoin, which was created as a joke on the 2013 cryptocurrency frenzy with the Shiba Inu dog breed as its logo. A deluge of cash thanks to government stimulus plans, speculation coupled with fear of missing out, a stubborn backing from Musk and some pure online fun thanks to social media's fondness for the Doge meme are some of the reasons behind Dogecoin's dream run that has seen the coin surge more than 20,000% in the past year.

"The Dogecoin craze started primarily with retail traders coming from social media platforms. The retail trading community seemed convinced that Dogecoin was going to pay $1 and for many, the fundamentals didn't matter," Edward Moya, senior market analyst at Oanda, told DW. Celebrity endorsements from Elon Musk and Mark Cuban in addition to Gene Simmons provided justification for many early investors and fueled the latest fervor.

In a major boost to Dogecoin's stardom, Musk's commercial rocket company, SpaceX, accepted payment for a lunar satellite mission in the cryptocurrency. The Dogecoin-funded mission scheduled for 2022 is called "DOGE-1 Mission to the Moon."

MANY PEOPLE ARE WONDERING if Dogecoin will be the next Bitcoin This has been one of the most searched cryptocurrency-related questions on Google over the past few months. Dogecoin and Bitcoin are two very different giants, even if the former is based on the same software code that underpins Bitcoin.

DOGECOIN CAN POTENTIALLY HAVE an infinite supply, meaning that those looking to stay invested in the coin for longer may see the value of their investment decrease over time. Bitcoin, on the other hand, has a fixed supply of 21 million units, making it scarce and, in turn, more valuable, just like gold and diamonds, which also have a limited supply.

WHILE DOGECOIN WAS CONCEIVED to be a cryptocurrency for "jokers," Bitcoin was always designed to be a decentralized digital currency, an alternative to central bank-controlled fiat money. Many diehard fans of digital currencies see Dogecoin and the speculative fervor surrounding it as undermining their broader goal of bringing cryptocurrencies like Bitcoin and Ethereum into the mainstream. They say memecoin is just a speculative asset, with few institutional investors backing it.

Although Dogecoin has come a long way from its satirical origins to being a popular peer-to-peer cryptocurrency, it is nowhere near threatening Bitcoin's dominance. Its $70 billion valuation is just a fraction of Bitcoin's $1 trillion.

"Dogecoin is cryptokindergarten. It was created to have fun and also illustrate how cryptocurrencies work," Jeff Gallas, founder of the German Bitcoin Foundation, told DW. "So it's good to start, perhaps, to get informed about how cryptocurrencies work and not take it too seriously."

## DOGECOIN, **a good investment**

DOGECOIN FANS SWEAR BY IT, touting it as a cryptocurrency of the future with Musk anointing it as the "people's crypto." Its low transaction fees and large supply make it convenient for netizens to use the coin to tip online content such as bloggers and creators on Reddit and YouTube. It is also easier to mine, the process of creating new Bitcoins through complex mathematical problems, which means transactions with Dogecoin can be processed faster than with Bitcoin.

Others see Dogecoin as a highly speculative and risky investment, much more so than Bitcoin or Ethereum. Despite Musk's support for the currency, none of his companies have publicly invested in Dogecoin so far, unlike Bitcoin.

Even Musk has urged people to "invest with caution" and said it was unwise to invest a life savings in cryptocurrencies, which for now should be considered speculative.

"Dogecoin is unlikely to become the preferred currency used by U.S. businesses, but for now retail interest could see Dogecoin suffer a fate similar to GameStop," Moya said. Dogecoin's valuation is not justifiable, but retail support seems relentless and could keep its prices elevated well above a justifiable valuation.

We close with three words from Elon Musk, posted on his social network Twitter last Dec. 20, 2020, and which shot up Dogecoin's value by 25%: @elonmusk "One world: Doge" 5:30 am - Dec. 20, 2020

# SEVEN

# GENERATING PASSIVE INCOME WITH DOGECOIN USING OTHER CRYPTOCURRENCIES

As you may have noticed throughout the development of the book, currently there are several ways to generate money with cryptocurrencies, there are many opportunities. While there are some that are more risky (and depend on your ability) such as trading, DeFi platforms, etc, there are others that are more recommended and less risky, such as Hodl (hold) of a cryptocurrency and wait for its price to rise, although this earning model is absolutely passive and speculative, as it is a long-term strategy, we have other strategies that can also help you generate passive income, as is the strategy that I will present below.

This strategy has existed for many years, it is widely used by banks today, although in a higher percentage of profit, this is to generate interest with your assets.

In the world of cryptocurrencies this modality already exists and is led by one of the most reliable companies in the environment: BlockFi, which is backed by the Gemini exchange and people as recognized in the environment as Anthony Pompliano.

BlockFi allows us to transfer our funds to the platform and generate an annual interest that goes from 6% (for cryptocurrencies such as Bitcoin) or almost 10% with stablecoins (which are cryptocurrencies that are 1 to 1 with the dollar, such as USDT and USDC to name a few).

If you are interested in this modality, you can open a BlockFi account at the following link and earn $250 worth of Bitcoin for free:

## Get your BONUS on BlockFi here

IN CASE you are reading this book in print version you can scan the following QR code with your cell phone:

# EIGHT

# THE MOST IMPORTANT THINGS TO KEEP IN MIND WITH DOGECOIN

To conclude this book, I would like to thank you for taking the time to read it, I wanted to clarify a few things before finishing.

Many people have tried dabbling in cryptocurrencies, some with success others with moderate results, but all with results in the end, the important thing is that you keep in mind that the cryptocurrency market is a highly manipulated market, which is why I recommend that you always pay attention to the indicators that you can see in TradingView, see the signals it sends you, continue learning about trading, if you are interested you can dedicate yourself to them, but if not you can dedicate yourself to do HODL (the meaning of this within the Cryptocurrencies is related to buy coins when there is a significant decline (for example if Bitcoin is at $58000 and drops to $36500 that's where you buy and go buying as it goes down, never when it goes up, this is known as Dollar Cost Averaging is a strategy widely used in the trading environment) and keep those cryptocurrencies for years until they double, triple or quadruple their value, it is not uncommon in the environment, as well have done those early adopters who bought Bitcoin when it was worth $0.006 cents, did HODL for 14 years and when Bitcoin reached its all-time high of $20,000 dollars in 2017 and $60,000 in 2021, sold everything and became millionaires. But as always, choose the method you like best and follow it at your own risk.

Finally, I would like to know your comments to continue to nurture this book and to help many more people, for them would you help us by leaving a review of this book, in order to continue providing great books to you, my readers, which I appreciate very much.


LINKS **for you**

Check crypto prices here:

https://coinmarketcap.com/

Get free Bitcoin:

**Get free bitcoin here**

Get your BlockFi bonus here:

https://blockfi.com/?ref=76971ae9

Trading crypto:

**Binance**

**Bitmex**

Buy Crypto:

**Coinbase**

**CEX.IO**

**Changally**

**Localbitcoins**

Donde guardar tus criptomonedas:

**Get the Trezor Model T here**

**Get the Trezor Model ONE here**

**Get a Ledger Nano S here**

More trading tools at:

transmit all the current education and information based on the most traded and known cryptocurrencies (the books will be updated every year as progress is made).


- VOLUME 1: Bitcoin in a Nutshell
    - Volume 2: Ethereum in a Nutshell
    - Volume 3: Dogecoin in a Nutshell
    - Volume 4: Cardano ADA in a Nutshell
    - Volume 5: DEFI for Beginners

## NINE

# DO YOU WANT TO FURTHER DEEPEN YOUR KNOWLEDGE?

If you found this book very useful, let me tell you that this book is part of the collection "Criptomonedas en Español" where we want to

www.TradingView.com

Best regards
Sebastian Andres